BAD PETS

HALL *of* SHAME

BAD PETS

HALL *of* SHAME

ALLAN ZULLO

Scholastic Inc.

ISBN 978-1-338-18658-1

10   21

Printed in the U.S.A.   40
First printing 2017

Book design by Charice Silverman

To the Wartowski kids—Annika, Clara, and Jackson—
who will always be Hall of Famers
in everything they do.
—A.Z.

CONTENTS

Oh, the Shame of It All

The animal kingdom teems with pets and wild beasts whose outrageous, ridiculous, or mortifying actions have brought embarrassment to all creatures big and small. These wacky troublemakers deserve the ultimate notoriety—as members of the Bad Pets Hall of Shame.

There is no actual museum or building dedicated to animal absurdity. If there were, it might stretch several blocks to accommodate all the awards and memorabilia for the goofs and gaffes, bloopers and blunders that dogs, cats, and other animals have committed over the years.

This book attempts to honor a recent sampling of the wackiest, head-scratchingest (yes, that's a made-up word, so don't use it in your next book report), scatter-brained moments perpetrated by pets.

The selection process for which animals were lucky enough (or unlucky enough, depending on your point of view) to be inducted into the Hall involved certain standards. For each incident up for consideration, the author asked such questions as: "Is it true?", "Will it make the reader laugh?", and "Is it so outlandish or silly that the reader will shake his or her head in disbelief?" If the answer was yes to all those questions, then the shameful moment had an excellent chance of making the cut.

Among the two-legged, four-legged, finned, and winged creatures inducted into the Bad Pets Hall of

Shame are: the delinquent doggy duo who went for a joyride on their own in a pickup truck and crashed into a riverbank; the wacky pet kangaroo who stole women's underwear off clotheslines; the impish kitten who turned on the water faucet full blast and flooded an entire animal shelter; the hungry bear who broke into a bakery and devoured two dozen fresh pies—and then grabbed two more for takeout; and the pair of pet llamas who sparked a wild chase—shown live on national television—involving cops, lasso-twirling citizens, and pursuers in golf carts.

With this book, animals now have a place to claim some fame from their shame.

BAD PETS

HALL *of* SHAME

THE "SLY AS A FOX" ★ AWARDS ★

For brazenly stealing humans' possessions, the Bad Pets Hall of Shame inducts the following:

PEPPI

CHIHUAHUA

SADIE

YORKSHIRE TERRIER

Peppi and Sadie teamed up to steal a car and go for a joyride. It didn't end well. They crashed the vehicle into a Walmart. Their canine car caper made national news.

It all unfolded one summer day in 2016 when their owner, Fatima Rowe, took them for a drive to the store in Wayne, West Virginia. Because she had only a few things to buy and it was hot outside, she left the dogs in her older-model Ford Crown Victoria with the windows up, engine running, and air conditioning on to keep them cool. Little did she suspect her pets would turn into doggy delinquents.

While she was in Walmart, Peppi and Sadie did what they always did when they were alone—have fun. On this occasion, having fun meant stealing the car. Apparently, Peppi, whom Rowe described as the more rowdy of the two dogs, bounced around the front seat until the gear selector on the side of the steering column was knocked out of park and into neutral. The car began rolling forward on the slightly sloped parking lot.

Then, according to witnesses, Sadie took over. She jumped over to the driver's seat and, while standing on her hind legs, placed her paws on the steering wheel. Peppi was now riding shotgun. Walmart's security cameras caught the dogs' free ride, showing Sadie turning the car slightly to the left as the vehicle headed toward the store.

A witness told WSAZ-TV, of Huntington, West Virginia, that she was standing in front of the store when she noticed a car start moving from its parking space. Because the car was slowly rolling straight toward her, she thought the driver was someone she knew who was teasing her.

That is, until she had a good look at the driver—and saw it wasn't a person, but a dog. It was Sadie. The woman stepped out of the way in time and then watched in disbelief as the car gently crashed into the front of the store.

Acting like a typical car thief when a joyride ends, Peppi decided to hightail it out of there. He pressed a button on the passenger's side armrest that lowered the power window. Then he jumped out of the car, leaving his accomplice to take the rap.

A Walmart employee paged shoppers and asked that the owner of a Crown Victoria come to the front of the store. When Rowe identified herself, the employee explained what had happened. "I couldn't believe that [Peppi and Sadie] had done it," Rowe told WSAZ.

A bystander told Rowe, "[Sadie] was driving the car." Recalled Rowe, "I thought, 'She can't drive.'" Besides, the only license Sadie had was a dog tag.

Fortunately, Rowe was able to retrieve Peppi. Because there was hardly any damage to the car or the building, no charges were filed by the officer who responded to the scene.

After WSAZ aired the story and posted it on Facebook, the station received dozens of comments from viewers. One person said Sadie "had to be texting" while driving. Another wrote, "She was just having a *ruff* day."

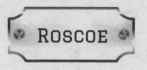

ROSCOE

LUNA

YELLOW LABRADOR RETRIEVER

BORDER COLLIE

Roscoe and Luna wound up in the doghouse after carjacking their owner's pickup, going on a wild ride for several blocks, and then crashing the vehicle into a riverbank.

In 2014, the partners in crime were left inside their owner's truck, which was parked on a hill near downtown Tulsa, Oklahoma. After about fifteen minutes, they somehow put the gear selector in neutral. They were ready to roll.

With Roscoe and Luna behind the wheel, the vehicle careered down the street for three blocks during rush hour. It zoomed across busy four-lane Riverside Drive without colliding into startled motorists and then barreled across a popular path, where runners and pedestrians scattered out of the way. The ride came to an abrupt end when the truck slammed into the bank of the Arkansas River, proving Roscoe and Luna weren't good drivers. Heck, the dogs couldn't even parallel *bark*.

"I got around to the front of the house where the truck was, and it's, like, not there," said the dogs' owner, Scott, who declined to give his last name. He told

FOX23 News, "I was, like, 'Did I get towed?' and I just thought, 'No, it didn't.'" He soon learned it was much worse than that, thanks to his two pets.

"Two boys on skateboards [saw] the vehicle leave in front of the residence, and they did try to catch up with it with no luck," Tulsa firefighter Clay Ayers told the TV station. After giving up the chase, the boys watched the dogs and the pickup narrowly avoid traffic and joggers before crashing into the riverbank.

Four witnesses called police to report the runaway truck, which had gathered "pretty good speed" down the hill to the river, Tulsa Police Department spokeswoman Jill Roberson told reporters. "When the fire department arrived, they were looking around for the driver, but no one was in the front but the dogs," she said.

Roscoe and Luna were unharmed (after all, their muscles were made of *steal*). The truck, however, sustained extensive damage. The crash also tied up traffic for three hours.

Police declined to issue the dogs a ticket for reckless driving. But it was still a bone of contention for Scott, who lamented, "It was an expensive joyride."

★

Honorable Mention: In 2016, a yellow Labrador retriever drove off in a semitrailer that was pulling a full load. The dog, apparently, wasn't. The truck traveled about one hundred yards before crashing into a tree and a parked car.

The canine was a travel companion of a long-distance trucker who had stopped at a Kwik Trip in Mankato, Minnesota. The driver had left the cab with the engine running to go into the store.

The Lab then hopped into the driver's seat, accidentally knocking the gearshift so the semi began to move forward. The truck traveled through the parking lot, crossed a street, and jumped a curb. With the dog still behind the wheel, the semi toppled a small tree and struck a car parked a few feet away. The Lab was not hurt. The *Mankato Free Press* published a photo of the dog leaning out of the driver's side window, surveying the damage. The canine no doubt got the *freight* of his life.

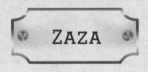

ZAZA

TORTOISESHELL ORIENTAL CAT

Zaza couldn't resist stealing stuffed animals and toys from the neighbors. During a one-month crime spree, she swiped seventeen cuddly figures and brought them back to her befuddled owner, who couldn't understand what they were doing in her house.

The wily five-year-old feline left at night through the cat flap and scoured the neighborhood, searching for plush toys to filch. She sneaked through open windows and doggy doors, creeping inside other people's residences until she found her treasure. Then, even if the stuffed animal was bigger than she was, she dragged it out of the victim's house and brought it to her owner's home.

For one bizarre month in 2013, Zaza's owner, Daisy Ayliffe, of London, England, would wake up every day or so and find a teddy bear or other stuffed animal outside her bedroom door. She didn't know if it came from a creepy intruder, a secret admirer, or her boyfriend.

"I came home one day, and there were three massive teddy bears in the house," Ayliffe told the *Daily Mail*. She thought Zaza had stolen them, but she wasn't sure because she hadn't seen the cat in possession of the stuffed animals. Besides, the teddy bears were larger than Zaza, making the owner wonder how her pet could be the perpetrator.

The cool cat's run of *purrfect* burglaries took a hit when she was caught in the act. "I was on the phone [with] my friend who was saying maybe an intruder is bringing the teddies in because the cat wouldn't be bringing in such massive teddy bears," Ayliffe recalled.

"Then at that moment, the cat came through the cat flap with a giant [stuffed] doughnut" and left it triumphantly on the kitchen floor.

"I thought, 'This is really weird.' Then another day I thought she had caught a mouse because she was playing with something squeaking. Then I realized it was a squeaking teddy bear, and it has just gone on from there.

"I woke up one day with an Eeyore [stuffed animal] in my bed. I've also had a hanging mobile from a baby's pram [stroller]. She has brought loads of them that are bigger than she is, and she's climbing along fences with these teddy bears. She must have really strong jaws."

Zaza's pilfered items range from a stuffed Roman gladiator to a Winnie the Pooh doll. "She used to leave them outside the bedroom door," the owner said. "It was really funny."

Zaza had racked up a *paw-some* number of burglaries by the time she came home with her seventeenth and final stolen teddy bear. She presented it to Ayliffe and her boyfriend while they were enjoying dinner in the backyard. "A big brown teddy bear fell on our table," Ayliffe recalled. The cat had lugged it from her latest victim, climbed a fence with it, and dropped it on the couple, whose table was next to the fence.

"It's sweet the way she offered the teddies as gifts, but she's a bonkers cat," said Ayliffe. "My sister said the neighbors would be really cross, but it's not my fault the cat is a thief."

Zaza's days of larceny ended when the couple moved to an apartment where the backyard was bordered by a wall too high for her to climb.

"We have been able to stop her burgling," Ayliffe told the newspaper. "Although, in the first week in our new flat, the little boy in the flat above us lost his teddy bear when it fell out the window. Zaza found it within seconds. She came rushing into our new flat with it in her mouth."

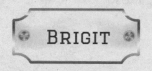

BRIGIT

TONKINESE CAT

Brigit was like many crafty cat burglars who specialize in what they snatch. For her, it wasn't money, jewelry, or electronics. Her specialty was men's underwear and socks. *No kitten.*

During a two-month period in 2016 in her new neighborhood in Hamilton, New Zealand, Brigit swiped eleven pairs of boxer briefs and more than fifty socks—many of them pairs—and brought them home to her owner, Sarah Nathan. "It's all men's," Nathan told the *New Zealand Herald*. "It's really, really weird. She's got really specific taste."

The six-year-old cat was less picky in her previous neighborhood. "In our last house, she'd bring home a bit of everything—men's undies, women's undies, togs [swimwear]," said Nathan. "She even brought home a hockey shin pad and a jumper [sweater]."

But once Brigit settled into her new digs and had time to case out the neighborhood, she chose to specialize in her *feline-ious* crimes. "Now she's decided menswear is her thing," Nathan told the newspaper. Underwear and socks became "an absolute obsession," she said. Nathan added, "A night does not go by without her bringing things home. I got up this morning, and there were another four socks in the house."

Brigit sometimes put her ill-gotten gains on or by her owner's bed. Other times she left them outside the cat flap. The furry thief often made sure to swipe socks in pairs, keeping victims on their toes for the cat burglar. "One sock will be at the front door and one will be at the back door, so she's obviously gone back to get the matching sock," Nathan said.

She added that one day, while gardening, she discovered "a whole bunch" of socks stuck in the fence. Nathan figured they became snagged when Brigit was returning from her nightly haul of socks and tried to jump over the fence with them.

The neighborhood crime spree ended when Nathan

and her pilfering pet moved to a two-acre property in the country. Before leaving, Nathan put together a *catalogue* of the stolen socks and underwear and tried to find their owners. She distributed flyers on her street and posted photos of Brigit's loot on Facebook to see if anyone recognized their missing items.

The socks varied in style, color, and length, including workers' socks, sport socks, and dress socks. There were black, gray, white, and striped socks—and, ironically, even several CAT brand socks. The boxer briefs were brightly colored and most were striped. Also displayed in the Facebook photo was Brigit's last haul—several boy's tighty-whities.

"I've got this massive bag [of stolen socks and underwear]," Nathan said. "You'd think someone would've noticed their items were missing. I feel so bad about it. Someone is spending a fortune on underwear."

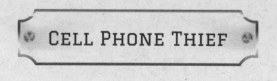

❖ CELL PHONE THIEF ❖

FOX

A wild fox stole a teenager's cell phone—and then mocked the victim by later texting a strange message. It might sound like a *phone-y* claim, but it's true.

Sixteen-year-old Lars Andreas Bjercke, of Oslo, Norway, downloaded an app claiming it could attract foxes by imitating the sound of a rabbit in distress. One night in 2012, Lars decided to test the app and went out into his backyard. Sure enough, a fox appeared and warily circled the yard. Using the app, the boy lured the fox over the next several nights.

Thinking the encounter would be cool if it were videotaped, he summoned his friend, Sigurd Grønvik Bachke, to record it on a subsequent night. Lars turned on the app and placed his phone in the middle of the street. Like clockwork, the fox showed up.

While Sigurd was recording the experience on his own smartphone, the fox tentatively approached Lars's phone, which was lying on the street and sounding like a dying rabbit. At first, the fox seemed afraid of the phone, but it soon crept close enough to smell it. Then the fox grew bolder and bit it. Suddenly, the fox grabbed the phone with its teeth and ran off into the bushes.

Although somewhat shocked, both boys began laughing as they chased after the thief. But he was faster than they were and quickly disappeared from view.

According to the Norwegian newspaper *Verdens Gang*, this was no ordinary fox, considering what the critter did next.

Having been robbed of his phone, Lars figured he could get it back by having Sigurd call it. That way they could follow the sound of the ringing and trace it. But the fox outsmarted them. When Sigurd called, the fox answered the phone! It was a close call.

"I heard something crunch as if the fox was fiddling with the phone," Sigurd told the newspaper. "I sat and listened for five minutes." Unfortunately for the lads, the sly fox wasn't talking. Instead, the thief was just taunting them, refusing to give up the phone's location.

After the boys searched the area without success, the fox teased them by appearing again—without the phone—before dashing off into the darkness.

Ah, but the four-legged crook wasn't finished tormenting Lars. Two days later, a friend of Lars received a text that came from the victim's stolen phone. "She sent me a message on Facebook and wondered if I got my mobile back," Lars told *Verdens Gang*. "She had received a text message with a bunch of letters and numbers from my phone number."

The text read: "jlv I øi\ a0ab 34348tu åaugjoi zølb-mosdji jsøg ijio sjiw."

The friend wondered why Lars would send such a weird message. Not having a fox-to-Norwegian option on Google Translate, Lars had no clue what the text meant. But he certainly knew who—or rather what—sent it. The larcenous fox.

Lars, who had the phone deactivated, told the newspaper, "At first we thought it was great fun, but it was a smartphone, so [the crime] was a bit sour."

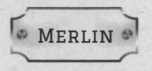

MERLIN

BURMESE CAT

Merlin was a wizard at making golf balls disappear. He stole them from a golf course, annoying players. And that's no lie.

His thievery became so blatant that the owners of the golf club had to create a special rule for golfers just to deal with the ball-swiping feline.

Merlin lived with his owner, Peter Bryson, in a bungalow about 100 yards from the Aldeburgh Golf Club in Suffolk, England. The cat always enjoyed playing with Ping-Pong balls, but in 2016, when he was two years old, he swatted those aside in favor of a driving ambition to steal golf balls from the nearby course. Bryson told the BBC that Merlin would bring home as many as six golf balls a day.

Ever since the club was founded in 1884, golfers there have had to deal with the usual hazards of the game, including bunkers, trees, and tricky winds. But after more than 130 years of fair play, golfers were victimized by a new challenge on the 408-yard fourteenth hole. That's where Merlin repeatedly carried out his shameless larceny.

The cat had to cross local gardens and a private road, then wriggle through a hedge to reach his secret hiding spot, where he lay in wait for a player to hit a golf ball onto the fairway. Once the ball stopped rolling, Merlin would dash from the rough, pounce on the ball, and scamper away with it while the helpless golfer watched in frustration.

One player told the *Daily Mail*, "The cat is very clever. He knows the best place to be is halfway down the fairway where most of the balls land. I have seen him run onto the fairway and grab one in his mouth before running off again."

Players' irritation came to a head in 2016 when Merlin repeatedly struck at the fourteenth hole during a tournament. Club official Melissa Baker told the paper that "quite a few members" had seen Merlin stealing balls. "Most take it in good humor, but others have taken it more seriously."

According to the *Daily Mail*, Bryson contacted the club after hearing rumors that some fed-up members were planning to harm Merlin if he continued his thieving ways. Officials reassured Bryson the rough comments were said in jest.

However, there were enough serious complaints about the cat that the club created a special rule approved by golf's governing body, The Royal and Ancient Golf Club of St. Andrews, to deal specifically with Merlin. A sign on the club's notice board warned: "A large brown Burmese cat has been seen picking up and carrying away golf balls in the vicinity of the fourteenth hole. Where this has been witnessed or when it is virtually certain that a ball has disappeared from the closely mown surfaces, a substitute ball may be dropped."

It informed players the cat should be considered an "outside agency" (meaning someone or something that has moved the ball other than the golfer or caddy). If the cat stole the player's ball, the golfer was allowed to play a substitute ball without a penalty from the spot where the crime took place. However, if Merlin stole the ball after the player hit it in the rough or out of bounds, the golfer had to take a penalty stroke.

Bryson told the newspaper, "I don't know what it is about golf balls, but Merlin just loves them." Golfers hoped Merlin would stop and *putt* his larceny behind him.

BENJI

KANGAROO

Benji the pet kangaroo leaped into the news in 2011 after going on an underwear-stealing rampage.

The two-year-old marsupial, owned by Petr Hlabovic, of Prague, Czech Republic, was no *pouch* potato. Benji was full of energy. So when he managed to escape from his enclosure, he bounced around the neighborhood.

Hopping from yard to yard, Benji, for whatever reason, began collecting women's lingerie that had been hanging on clotheslines. Women began to—ahem— *(w)underwear* their unmentionables went. Only when one victim looked out her kitchen window and saw Benji bounding off with her undies was the perpetrator identified. Some victims tried to catch him, but he gave them the slip.

A spokesperson for the police in Prague told reporters, "We had a call from the kangaroo's owner saying it had escaped. At the same time, we started getting reports of a number of thefts from washing lines."

Although it all sounded strange, the police didn't immediately jump to a conclusion. "We didn't think the reports [of the missing underwear and kangaroo] could possibly be related until the animal was caught red-handed," said the spokesperson.

Benji had several stolen lingerie items draped over his ear, pouch, and front leg when caught. "I'm very relieved to have him back," his owner said. "I've got no idea what he thought he was up to. He certainly didn't pick up the habit from me."

Benji's underwear-nabbing escapade was reported throughout the world—in news briefs.

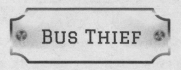

BUS THIEF

MONKEY

A wild street monkey went bananas and stole a bus.

Like many towns and cities in India, Pilibhit has its share of mischievous monkeys who like to swipe food off people's plates and snatch purses and cameras. This particular thief was one of those naughty simians. But he had a bigger crime in mind—none of this misdemeanor stuff. No, his dream felony was grand theft auto. Instead of a car, he set his sights on a bus.

As *The Times of India* stated, "The simian menace in the city took a turn for the absurd."

One day in 2015, a bus owned by the Uttar Pradesh State Road Transport Corporation (UPSRTC) was parked outside a station in Pilibhit. The driver was the only person in the vehicle, which was scheduled to leave thirty minutes later. Knowing he had time to kill, the driver ambled to the back row of the bus and took a nap.

That's when the monkey made his move. He quietly climbed onto the bus through an open door and hopped into the driver's seat. Seeing the key in the ignition, the hairy sneak knew this was a golden opportunity for a little monkey business. He turned the key, causing the engine to roar to life.

Maybe hearing the loud motor scared the monkey, because he shifted the bus into second gear. The bus lurched forward and headed away from the station.

The noise and movement immediately shook the driver awake. It took a moment before he realized that, yes, the bus was moving and, yes, that was indeed a monkey behind the wheel. While yelling at the thief, the driver ran down the aisle toward the front. This threw a monkey wrench in the crook's plan for a lengthy excursion in the stolen bus, so the simian fled.

The Times of India reported, "Passengers seeing the pilotless vehicle headed their way ran helter-skelter, while the duty staff at the [station] were unable to find the reason behind the disturbance." UPSRTC regional manager SK Sharma said, "The driver managed to regain control of the bus but not before it hit two parked buses.

"Monkeys have become a regular menace at bus stations and workshops, where they often fiddle with vehicles undergoing repair. They have also damaged closed-circuit TV cameras at stations. Three years back we were able to get rid of them with the help of municipal authorities, but they have returned."

The thief certainly made a monkey out of the driver.

★

Honorable Mention: A dolphin at SeaWorld in Orlando, Florida, stole a visitor's iPad. In 2016, a woman had taken out her device to snap a closeup photo of dolphins frolicking in a pool. She leaned over the two-foot-high barrier that surrounded the pool and held out her iPad for the photo of the animals.

To the crowd's surprise, the dolphin lunged from the surface and snatched the iPad right out of the startled woman's hands. Clenching the device in its teeth, the dolphin slid back into the water.

The woman was not amused and managed to retrieve her iPad—although having been in the salt water, the device was likely ruined. A visitor nearby who caught the attempted theft on video posted it on social media.

No one knows the *porpoise* of the crime. Was the dolphin camera shy, or did it wish to take pictures of people? Either way, the dolphin's finned friends showed their support for his actions: They splashed the tourists who were standing next to the iPad owner.

HERBERT "HERBIE" SPENCER

CAT

A cat named after a British philosopher probably should have been named after a thief—because that's what he was. And the victims were his loving human family.

Owner Phil Bailey, of Manitoba, Canada, had dentures. As he was preparing to shower one evening, he took out his teeth and placed them on the bathroom sink. On a 2008 post on Oprah.com, his wife, Glenda, explained, "He went for a clean towel, and when he came back, his teeth were missing. We searched for an hour, and they were nowhere to be found. He was forced to go to work for days without them."

Although they couldn't prove it, family members figured the culprit was Herbert Spencer, who was grinning like a Cheshire cat. Phil was gnashing his teeth (figuratively, of course, because he didn't have any).

The Baileys' son, Josh, told his high school marching band bandmates about the theft. One of his pals teased Phil, saying, "What's the matter, Mr. Phil, the cat got your teeth?"

Recalled Glenda, "Well, several days later, our son was watching TV and covered himself with an afghan. Lo and behold, the dentures were wrapped in the afghan. My son called my husband and told him he had just been bitten [by Phil's missing teeth].

"Two weeks later, Phil's watch was missing, and we found it in Herbie's secret hiding spot—the afghan. The afghan is long gone, and now Herbie has hiding spots we know nothing about, but we are certain when things are missing, Herbie has absconded with them!"

THE "BULL IN A CHINA SHOP"

★ CITATIONS ★

For causing outrageous damage or destruction,
the Bad Pets Hall of Shame inducts the following:

WATER FREAK

MIXED-BREED KITTEN

A naughty kitty at the Florida Humane Society in Pompano Beach turned on a water faucet at the shelter and left it running full blast for seventeen hours, flooding the building and causing thousands of dollars in damage.

Suspicion fell on the frisky six-month-old female kitten because she had a reputation for playing in the sink and batting at the faucet handle in a cat room.

In a 2016 afternoon, the staff made one last check of a room that served as the temporary home of about two dozen felines who were free to roam, play, and sleep there. All seemed quiet and secure. Later, with no one to stop her, the suspect hopped onto the sink, turned the faucet lever all the way on, then flew off the handle and watched the water show.

Throughout the afternoon and evening and into the early morning hours, the water flowed nonstop over the sink and onto the floor of the nonprofit's shelter. Humane Society president Carol Ebert felt a sinking feeling in her stomach when she received a call at 7:15 a.m., informing her that water was running out the back door of the facility.

When staff members arrived, they assumed a water pipe had burst. But when they looked for the cause of the flood, they discovered that the water faucet in the cat room had mysteriously been turned on.

The flood left three to four inches of standing water, damaging cabinets and walls of eight rooms, including the cat, examination, and quarantine rooms. The flood also ruined a large amount of cat food and litter. Fortunately, the felines in the cat room at the time were all high and dry because they stayed on countertops or on their sleeping perches. The six cats in the quarantine room weren't affected because their cages sat well above the water.

Because of mold and mildew, walls, counters, and cabinets had to be replaced. Foster families took in the shelter's cats, while workers repaired the damage, which was estimated at more than $5,000.

"It's quite a mess," volunteer Terry Arbour told the *Miami Herald*. "And we can't imagine what our next water bill is going to look like."

Although none of the cats confessed, the Humane Society felt confident the culprit in hot water was the mischief-making wet-behind-the-ears kitten with a fascination for faucets. The shelter declined to name her, perhaps because she was a juvenile.

"We can't be sure which cat did it, because we don't have cameras in there, but we have a good idea because there was one younger female cat who really liked playing in sinks," Arbour told the newspaper. "There was a tall spout [with a handle] in that sink that moves around, and the cat somehow was able to turn it on. It's possible there was collusion from others, but she probably had something to do with it."

Shortly after the flood, the suspect was adopted. Arbour said the staff warned the new owners that "this cat is intelligent enough to turn on water faucets." Hopefully, for the feline, bad memories of what she did won't come flooding back.

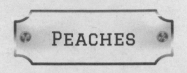

PEACHES

BICHON FRISE

To the British press, Peaches was England's most
destructive dog.

In 2016, the one-year-old pooch caused thousands
of dollars' worth of damage to her owner's home,
destroying clothes, books, door frames, and furniture—
including a couch that she demolished in three hours.

"Whatever she can get her paws on, she will chew,"
Sharon Johnston, of Warrington, Cheshire, England,
told the *Daily Mirror.* "And she doesn't just chew it a
bit. She leaves a path of destruction wherever she goes.
I don't know how such a small dog does so much
damage.

"She has eaten the entire sofa, chewed through the
lawn mower, the back door, the garden table and chairs,
and she tears the clothes down off the washing line. I've
not kept a tally, but [the cost of] clothes, shoes, and furniture that we've lost must be in the thousands.

"It is so shocking and I do get angry, but it is so
hard to shout at her when it is so hilarious. At first I'm
outraged, but then I can't help but crack up." She said
her children—Jack, 18, and Sophie, 14—laughed, too,
at their pet's destructive—and expensive—habit.

When Peaches was three days old, Johnston rescued her and then bottle-fed the puppy formula every two hours—even through the night—for more than a week. "We formed such a special bond," she said. The connection extended to her children. "Peaches is a member of the family—just like a third child, but way naughtier than either of them ever were."

Around six months old, Peaches—who had some poodle and bulldog in her—turned into a tiny terror. She chewed up Johnston's slippers and flip-flops, then graduated to Sophie's new sneakers and school shoes. The dog also tore into the kids' school bags and mangled their books. Five minutes after Johnston donned a new warm-up outfit, Peaches ripped the back seam clean open.

"I hoped it was a phase, but Peaches just got cheekier," Johnston told the British magazine *Real People*. "She'd leap up as I walked past, nipping at the seat of my black leggings before trying to yank them down. Living in our house was like being in a comedy sketch. I'd be running around the kitchen, trying to get away from Peaches before she pulled my trousers round my ankles and chewed them to shreds. All my leggings were punched with teeth marks, so my knickers [underwear] showed through. My handbags were torn to tatters, too."

In the backyard, Peaches would jump up and pull sheets and clothes off the clothesline. "I'd come outside to see her dragging sheets in the dirt," Johnston said. "Soon, I was doing three loads of wash a day—one wash to clean everything, and another two to get the muck out after Peaches had her fun. She wanted to gnaw the world."

One day, Johnston came home from shopping and found piles of sawdust everywhere. Peaches had chewed part of a door frame to splinters and gnawed at the plaster beneath.

Fearing that the dog would systematically destroy the house room by room, Johnston set up a lounge in the back of her home solely for her pet. It had a gate to keep Peaches from the rest of the residence. It also had doggy toys and bones and a $2,400 brown couch that had belonged to the kids' late grandmother. Peaches loved sleeping on it. Then again, maybe not.

After being gone for three hours, Johnston returned home to discover that Peaches had demolished the couch. "Peaches was barely visible beneath a mountain of sofa stuffing and brown fabric," Johnston said in *Real People*. "I could just see her black eyes peeping out from inside the sofa frame. She'd somehow stripped all the covers and stuffing right off, so only the wood frame remained. 'Oh, Peaches, how could you?' I cried. She'd eaten her way through an entire sofa in three hours! But Peaches was wagging her tail, looking at me as if to say, 'Aren't you proud of me, Mum?' As I lifted her out of the frame, I had to stifle a chuckle. I just couldn't understand how such a small dog had managed to wreak so much havoc."

Despite all the destruction, Johnston told the *Daily Mirror* the family never had an urge to get rid of the dog. "The way I see it is as long as she's okay and she's happy, then I am, too," she said. "The rest is just stuff that can be replaced. But nothing could ever replace Peaches."

★

Honorable Mention: Versace, Armani, and Coco—three whippets—became an internet sensation in 2015 after their owner posted a video of their handiwork. While the owner was at work, they had completely shredded his bed—sheets, blankets, pillows, and mattress—down to the box spring.

Paul "Fluff" Sinclair, of Mansfield, Victoria, Australia, came home to find his bed totally ripped apart by his three whippets. He recorded the scene on his cell phone and put it on Facebook and YouTube.

The video showed pieces of foam and bedding littering the stairway leading to Sinclair's bedroom. As the dogs ran up the stairs ahead of him, their owner exclaimed, "Goodness me! Look at all this mess! What have you been doing when I have been at work earning money to buy you treats?"

When he reached his bedroom, Sinclair shouted,

"Look what you have done to my bed!" As the dogs frolicked on the rubble, he moaned, "It's all gone! Look, you've gone all the way down to the springs . . . to China! You cheeky little whippets!" The angry tone in his voice told the dogs that he wasn't pleased. Their tails drooped because they knew they were *bed* to the bone.

It wasn't the first time they had turned into vandals. Sinclair told the local newspaper, the *Mansfield Courier*, that in the first four years the whippets had lived with him, they had destroyed two Chesterfield couches, a dozen pairs of shoes, four remote controls, numerous cushions, the front seat of his car, and a prized wood and leather Eames chair. Too many of his possessions had gone to the dogs.

JESS

BORDER COLLIE

Jess was a fool who rushed in where others feared to tread. She deliberately bit the tires of neighbors' cars, causing them to go flat.

During a six-month period in 2014, residents in a section of Brampton, Cumbria, England, were reporting to police that a vandal was puncturing the tires of their parked vehicles. A spokeswoman for the Cumbria Police Department confirmed ten reports of vandalism to tires during that time, though authorities believed many other victims failed to contact the police.

A mechanic at a local car garage who had replaced or repaired numerous punctured tires at a flat rate told the *Daily Mail*, "I was having to replace car tires every couple of weeks. Everyone thought it was someone with a knife."

Police constable Simon Amos investigated the crimes but had few clues to work with. The problem was deflating to neighbors who lived on one particularly hard-hit street, so they installed a security camera in an effort to catch the culprit.

After spending hours studying video, Amos blew open the case when the camera caught the criminal red-handed or, more accurately, red-pawed. The criminal was none other than that dirty dog, Jess, the border collie.

When Amos confronted the canine's owners, retirees Edward and Jean Morgan, the news punctured their view of their sweet, lovable three-year-old pooch. She had been tirelessly leading a double life as a vandal.

Video showed that whenever she was let off her leash during walks with her owners, she would trot over to parked vehicles and nip at the tires without the couple noticing. Sometimes her teeth sank deep enough into a tire to cause a slow leak, so the tire was flat by morning.

Confronted with the proof, "we are both just

mortified," Jean told the newspaper. "She is the most obedient and affectionate dog we have ever had, and it is just shocking to hear this terrible news. We are very distressed by what happened. I couldn't believe it when I saw the [security] footage.

"To think that Jess has done this has made me feel very sad. I have had six dogs over the last fifty years, and none has ever been like Jess. She is such a lovely dog and very spirited."

The couple reimbursed fellow residents for the damage that Jess caused at about $100 a pop. Since then, Jess was kept on a leash during walks. She was no longer a vandal because she was retired.

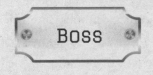

BOSS

FRENCH BULLDOG

Boss had no sense of history. He chewed up the baseball from the final out of the 2007 World Series.

At the time, Boss was the pet of Jon Papelbon, the Boston Red Sox ace relief pitcher. It was Papelbon who struck out Colorado Rockies batter Seth Smith to end Game 4 and clinch Boston's second World Series title in four years. After catching the third strike of the final out, Red Sox catcher Jason Varitek slipped the ball into his back pocket and celebrated on the field with his teammates. After the game, Varitek said he would give the historic ball to the team, but a few days later, he handed it over to Papelbon to keep.

The pitcher brought the ball to his home in Hattiesburg, Mississippi, for family and friends to admire. Boss always had a fascination with baseballs. He loved playing with them—and gnawing on them. So when he saw this particular hardball, well, he just had to have it.

"My dog ate it," Papelbon told the *Hattiesburg American*. "He plays with baseballs like they are his toys. He jumped up one day on the counter and snatched it. He likes rawhide. He tore that thing to pieces. I'll keep what's left of it."

Yep, Boss sure had a ball.

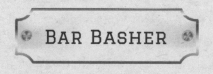

BAR BASHER

SQUIRREL

A squirrel went nuts and ransacked a bar, spilling gallons of beer on the floor and causing hundreds of dollars in damage. No one would have known he was the culprit if he hadn't lapped up some of the booze and become too drunk to leave.

Sam Boulter, who oversaw the Honeybourne Railway Club in Worcestershire, England, opened up the private club one evening in 2015 and thought hooligans had broken into the place. Puddles of beer had been spilled on the floor, glasses and bottles had been knocked off the shelves, and money and straws were scattered throughout the establishment. It looked like a scene from *Bar Wars*.

"When I opened the door, the bar was absolutely ransacked," he told the *Worcestershire News*. "At first I thought we'd been burgled, but I realized it was all still locked up. And that's when we saw the squirrel."

It looked like the same rodent who had sneaked into the club the previous day. "I had chased him through the bar," Boulter said. "He jumped over the counter, and I thought he'd gone out the door, but obviously he was still inside."

After the club had closed, the squirrel had his own happy hour. He *razed* the bar to a new level. He scampered on the shelves and across the counter, knocking over bottles, glasses, and other items. The intruder hit some of the bar's pumps, ruining several barrels of beer, and also turned on a tap of Irish ale, spilling the brew all over the floor.

Boulter said the club lost about $400 worth of beverages. "It is just one of those once-in-a-lifetime things—I hope!"

When Boulter spotted the squirrel after the mess,

the rodent was staggering out from a box of potato chips. "He was a bit slow moving when we found him the next evening, so he may have drank a bit of the beer—but only after he had completely ransacked the place."

Boulter told the *International Business Times*, "I've never seen a drunk squirrel before. He looked a bit worse for wear."

Boulter eventually shooed the squirrel out the window. With the help of two customers, he spent an hour cleaning up the mess.

The club has a sign stating no dogs or other pets are allowed. It goes for squirrels, too.

HOME DOG, DA NAILS, SQUEAKY FEETS, 2-TOES TODD

RACCOONS

Four masked bandits broke into an art gallery and caused havoc before police nabbed them.

The artful dodgers had been raiding the Inscapes Gallery in Newport, Oregon, after closing time for several nights in 2015. The raccoons, who lived in the hills behind the gallery, were too small and sneaky to set off the burglar alarm.

Owner Cris Torp told Portland TV station KPTV

that the raccoons had been a problem for a long time. They would climb the exterior stairs to the top of the building and enter through a roof vent that led to a crawl space in the gallery. Once inside, they turned paintings on the walls cockeyed and knocked over artwork. After the vent was sealed, the invaders gained entry through another vent until that one was closed off, too.

What no one realized at the time was that the four critters were already in the crawl space when the owner sealed the second vent, so they became trapped in the gallery. Rather than worry about how they were going to escape, the *ra-goons* continued to vandalize the place. But they slipped up when a passerby spotted the four rascals in the front window and called the cops shortly after midnight.

"We were already in bed when we got this call [from the police]," Torp told the TV station. "They said it's going to be horrible because these raccoons are in the gallery."

When Torp arrived, paintings were crooked, shelves were cleared of artwork, and a few pieces were chipped. The gallery displayed many crystal art pieces, and the owner was relieved his place wasn't the scene of *glass destruction*.

"They'd tried to rearrange some artwork, and they were by a balsam wood boat that was made by a local artist, and that survived the onslaught," Torp added.

The Newport Police Department seized the intruders and took photos of them, which were posted on its Facebook page with this account:

"Four masked bandits burglarized Inscapes Gallery on SW Bay Blvd recently. Officers responded to a report of suspicious activity after midnight and cornered the suspects immediately upon entering the business. The suspects, known only by their street names of 'Home Dog,' 'Da Nails,' 'Squeaky Feets,' and '2-Toes Todd,' attempted to elude officers on scene. After a brief scuffle, all suspects were captured without further incident or injuries.

"'Squeaky Feets' told officers they had no intention of taking anything from the gallery; they were only trying to straighten a few pieces of art on the wall. Tell it to the judge, 'Feets.' Tell it to the judge."

❂ ELEAZAR ❂

GREYHOUND

Eleazar liked to sink her fangs into whatever interesting tasty morsel she could find—including her owner's false teeth.

The dog was a favorite of greyhound race trainer

Keiron Butler, of Goodna, Queensland, Australia. Eleazar, who had made news in 2015 when she birthed a litter of fourteen pups (who all survived), lived inside Butler's home, unlike his other greyhounds, who slept outside. One evening in 2016, Eleazar, a retired racer, was resting next to her owner while he ate pizza and watched a soccer match on television.

When Butler was ready for bed, he took out his dentures. "I usually put them in the cupboard, but this time I left them on the pizza tray with some leftover pizza," Butler told the *Queensland Times*. "About three o'clock in the morning, I heard the dog going 'crunch, crunch, crunch.' I thought, 'She's got a bit of my pizza, but I didn't think it was that crunchy.'

"The next morning I got up to look after my dogs and went to put my teeth in, but I couldn't find them." He searched everywhere in the house and finally located them—or what was left of them. "I found splinters of teeth all over the [living] room floor, and the teeth disintegrated into 5,000 pieces with the pizza."

Butler said when he discovered what the dog had done to his false teeth, he just patted her, explaining, "I can't lock her out of the house." In her racing days, she had won him money—and his heart. "She's my mate, my traveling companion," he told the newspaper. "I can't knock the dog. All she wanted was a piece of my pizza. I always leave some pizza there for her, and she must have thought my teeth were part of it. She is used to eating bones, so the false teeth probably tasted like bones."

In recalling the story of his chewed-up false teeth, Butler talked to a reporter with the help of some old army-issue dentures. "I was in the army and used to get my teeth knocked out playing [soccer] and in fights, so they made me a set about thirty years ago," Butler said. "They were sitting in my cupboard. They'll do for the time being. I've stuck them together with some super-glue, and I'll use those until one of my dogs can win a race so I can use the money to get a new set."

A friend of Butler's posted a story on Facebook about the chewed-up false teeth and included a photo of Eleazar's toothless owner. Thousands of people saw it. "I got phone calls from all over, even from a dental technician in Sydney who wants to make me a new set," Butler told the paper.

Eleazar had made him a local celebrity. When Butler walked into his favorite bar right after the story broke, all the patrons greeted him with big smiles—of wax candy false teeth.

★

Honorable Mention: A 100-pound pit bull named Champ, known as a great family dog, once bared his teeth—well, actually, he bared his owner's teeth. According to a 2012 blog from HealthPark Dentistry in

Tipp City, Ohio, the dog's owner ate some barbecued ribs, relaxed on the couch, and, before falling asleep there, took out his dentures.

"His son came in about 1:00 a.m., and good ol' Champ came to the door to greet him—wearing his Dad's denture!" the blog said. "Being a good son, he took the denture from Champ and put it up in the container in the bathroom where it's always kept."

Apparently, the scent of the barbecue sauce on the denture was so appealing to the dog that he gnawed on it. Later that morning, the son told his dad what Champ had done.

His father called dentist Charles "Chuck" Smith for help because the denture looked ruined, though Champ at least had the decency not to eat any of the teeth. Dr. Smith was able to rebuild the entire back of the denture and added the pink gum section. The newly formed, relined denture cost the owner $400, compared to $1,300 for a new denture.

The blog stated, "Our patient said now he knows that Champ really loves barbecue—and the guys at work are still laughing."

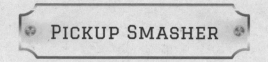

PICKUP SMASHER

HIPPOPOTAMUS

A hippo with a bad attitude toward smartphones made it clear he didn't want anyone taking video of him. So when the driver of a pickup truck started recording the hippo, the beast went into road-rage mode—ramming the vehicle and crushing the front end.

Wikus Ceronie was driving near Kruger National Park in South Africa when he noticed a hippo on the bridge. "There were people walking around in the nearby vicinity, so I automatically assumed this hippo was used to humans," Ceronie told LatestSightings.com, a website that chronicles encounters with wild animals. "I was quite fascinated by this, so I took out my phone to start filming."

The hippo was in no mood for cameras, so it snapped. "Suddenly the hippo turned and just started charging," Ceronie recalled. "This was terrifying for me because I realized I had nowhere to go and no time to do it."

Hippos may not look like it, but they are among the most dangerous and aggressive mammals on earth—and known to kill people if provoked or threatened. In addition to having massive teeth up to twenty inches long, they can run fourteen miles an hour on land.

This particular hippo had plenty of big teeth and could run fast. He charged directly at Ceronie, who was frozen in fear inside his pickup. "I braced myself as I realized he wasn't going to stop," Ceronie told the website. "He hit the [pickup] head on and then tried biting it. I guess after that he decided he had won because he just turned around and left."

Ceronie felt lucky the head-to-head encounter wasn't worse. "Beside me was a fifty-meter drop, so had he hit me on the side, I have no doubt the car would have rolled down the embankment. Even though there was damage done to the bonnet [hood] of my vehicle and the door couldn't open, I'm grateful there were no serious injuries at the end of day."

It was nice of the victim not to be too *hippo-critical*.

THE "HOLY COW!"
★ BADGES ★

For creating unnecessary trouble and mischief, the Bad Pets Hall of Shame inducts the following:

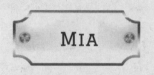

MIA

CHESAPEAKE BAY RETRIEVER

Mia stabbed her owner in the arm with a knife, sending the woman to the hospital. But the dog didn't mean to do it.

The one-and-a-half-year-old retriever, who was rather big for her age, belonged to Celinda Haynes of Hudson, Colorado. "[Mia] likes to grab whatever she can to get people to play with her," Haynes's daughter, Chanda Stroup, told TV station Denver7.

One day in 2016, Mia climbed onto the kitchen counter and grabbed a paring knife with her teeth. She clenched the handle so the blade was pointing out of her mouth. When Haynes saw what the dog had done, the woman set out several doggy treats on the floor, hoping they would make Mia drop the knife.

Mia wanted the treats but wasn't willing to give up the knife, apparently because she thought she looked sharp. As the dog went for the goodies, she took a shortcut, leaning over Haynes's outstretched arm and accidentally stabbing the owner, which wasn't a very *knife* thing to do.

Stroup told the TV station that when it happened, her mother said, "I need to go to the hospital. Mia just cut my arm with a knife!"

Stroup rushed her mother to the Platte Valley Medical Center, where Haynes received several stitches to close a four-inch-by-quarter-inch gash. When she told the medical staff that her dog had stabbed her, they didn't believe her and called law enforcement officers, who didn't buy her story, either. Who ever heard of a dog stabbing its owner?

"When dispatch said that there was a person who was stabbed by a dog, I had to make sure I heard that correctly," Deputy Marshal Zach Johnson told Denver TV station Fox31. "Of course, my initial thought was, 'What's really going on here?'"

Suspecting this might be domestic violence, deputies questioned Haynes's husband, who was at work at the time of the incident. They visited the hospital to question Haynes and then went to her home, where they found blood splattered across the kitchen floor. Upon further investigation, all evidence pointed to Mia.

"Obviously, we're not charging Mia with anything because she's a dog," Johnson said.

"Everybody has had quite a laugh about it," Haynes told Fox31.

After the incident, Mia was still trying to run off with kitchen knives. "She even pulls them out of the knife block," Haynes said. "Anything for me to chase her, she'll do it."

★

Honorable Mention: Trigger, a ten-year-old chocolate Labrador retriever, was aptly named. She accidentally shot her owner in the foot.

The dog was by the side of her owner, Allie Carter, of Avilla, Indiana, who was hunting waterfowl at Tri-County Fish and Wildlife Area in 2015. When Carter placed her loaded 12-gauge shotgun on the ground, she forgot to put on the safety. That was a resounding mistake. Trigger walked over and stepped on the weapon's trigger. The gun went off and shot Carter point-blank in the left foot. She was treated at the hospital and released later the same day and quickly recovered. For Trigger, it was her one shot at *shame*.

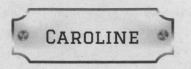

CAROLINE

BLACK LABRADOR RETRIEVER

Caroline made a big splash in the news in 2015 after she crashed a pickup truck into a backyard swimming pool.

Her owners, Michael and Ruth Smith, of Erwin, North Carolina, brought their dog with them as they rode in their 1988 Dodge Ram to the grocery store. After they bought their groceries, the couple climbed into their pickup and greeted their dog, who had been patiently waiting for them inside the vehicle.

Ruth started the truck and pulled out of the parking space when something spooked Caroline. "When she gets scared, she will go down on the floorboard of the truck," Michael told Raleigh TV station WRAL. The ninety-pound retriever became a retreater and dived at Ruth's feet, pinning the woman's right foot on the accelerator.

The pickup raced across the parking lot as Ruth valiantly steered clear of shoppers and their vehicles. Meanwhile, Michael leaned down and tried to pull Caroline off the gas pedal, but she weighed too much. "Before I could reach her, we were wide open," Michael told the TV station. "We were probably going 50 to 55 miles per hour."

Hearing Ruth and Michael screaming and the truck's engine roaring, Caroline was too frightened to budge. By now, the pickup had reached the other side of the parking lot. Unable to stop, Ruth steered the truck toward a wooden fence. "I didn't know what else to do," she told WRAL.

The runaway vehicle plowed through the fence, zoomed across a backyard, and splashed into a swimming pool before coming to a stop in the shallow end. Michael, who at the moment of impact was still bent under the dashboard trying to shove Caroline, recalled, "We hit the water, and I'm going, 'Where in the name of God is this water coming from?'"

The pool owner, John McNamara, was in the kitchen with his wife and was *lab-ergasted* when he saw the pickup in his pool. McNamara, who had had open-heart surgery three months earlier, joked to WRAL that he told his wife, "I'm going to have another heart attack here."

Water day it turned out for the canine and her owners. Caroline and the Smiths scrambled out of the pickup, which was totaled. Michael had a few cuts on his hands, but otherwise no one, including the dog, was hurt. "I hate that it happened to their pool, but I think that it might have saved our lives," Michael said.

Caroline's owners forgave her for their wet and wild experience.

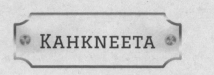 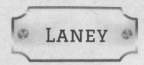

LLAMAS

It was a llama drama, a llamapalooza, a llama-mama-mia.

Whatever people on social media, on cable news, and in newspapers called it, Kahkneeta and Laney created a brief nationwide sensation when they ran amok in a suburb of Phoenix, Arizona, in 2015. TV crews on the ground and in the air broadcast live the two llamas' wild dash for freedom. Like juking and jiving basketball players, the two dodged handlers, cops, passersby, and lasso-flinging pursuers trying to catch them. The dynamic duo stopped traffic on busy streets, startled shoppers and residents on sidewalks, and captured the attention of the internet.

It wasn't supposed to happen that way. Bob Bullis and his wife, Karen Freund, who owned nine pet llamas, were bringing three of the animals—Kahkneeta, Laney, and Alejandro—to the Carillons, an assisted-living facility in the retirement community of Sun City, for residents to see and pet as a form of therapy. The normally mild-mannered animals became spooked when the door to the trailer transporting them unexpectedly opened before it came to a stop in front of the home. The three llamas bolted out of the transport . . . and the chase was on.

Alejandro gave up right away while his rebellious comrades performed their own version of *The Great Escape*. It turned into quite a spectacle, watched live by millions of people streaming the escapade on Twitter, Facebook, and local and national newsfeeds.

Pursuers chased them on foot and in golf carts, police cruisers, pickups, and bicycles. Cooks at the facility ran after them while holding heads of lettuce, trying to entice them to stop for a snack. Kahkneeta, a five-year-old white llama, sprinted ahead of the shorter, one-year-old dark-furred Laney. The pair often sprinted into oncoming traffic as people and Maricopa County sheriff's deputies approached them with arms outstretched. Weaving here and there, sidestepping this way and that, ducking and darting, the two llamas made fools out of everyone who tried to catch them.

"During the hour-long chase, the animals dodged cars as they crossed Thunderbird Road multiple times, disobeying pedestrian and vehicular laws and forcing those who were following them through neighborhoods to run in circles," the *Arizona Republic* reported.

This being Arizona, several persons with ropes showed up and figured they could snare the runaways with lassos, *no probllama*. Laney was the first to be lassoed by two men near 103rd Avenue. Kahkneeta remained on the loose for another fifteen minutes, still looking like a live stuffed animal—a *dolly llama*. But she was finally lassoed by a guy riding in the bed of a pickup truck that had been tailing the animal. Kahkneeta bucked and shook in defiance but then gave up and returned to her owners without any more fuss. Neither animal nor human was hurt in the zany pursuit.

Although the chase was over, the fun was only beginning on social media, which generated hundreds of hilarious memes picturing the llamas with such captions as "The Fast and the Furriest," "Thellma and Llouise," and "Como se llama?" (Spanish for *What is your name?*). A TV station captioned the video of the pursuit as a "Sllow speed chase." On Twitter, the hashtag #llamas became a trending topic worldwide, spurring hundreds of thousands of tweets, including hashtags #llamasontheloose and #llamadrama.

Even the NFL got in the act. The Arizona Cardinals football team tweeted that it "agreed to one-year deals with the #llamasontheloose. Each llama will earn 2,340 lbs. of hay." The Tampa Bay Buccaneers were impressed with Kahkneeta's running skills, tweeting, "Gotta love how well [s]he avoids the defense . . . And with the first pick in the draft, the @ TBBuccaneers pick the white llama."

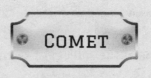

COMET

WOLF DOG

Comet could be the poster child (or canine, in this case) for the old expression, "Let sleeping dogs lie." For more than a dozen years, he had slept on the sidewalk near a busy intersection, fooling people into thinking he was dead.

The dog loved to snooze motionless flat on his back with his legs spread out on the sidewalk near the corner of Quebec Street and East Third Avenue in Vancouver, British Columbia, Canada. To passersby who had not seen him before, he looked like a dead or dying dog. Time and again, they winced in heartbreak, rushed to his aid, or called for help.

"It's constant, all day, every day," his owner, Lisa Dyer, told the CBC in 2016. "We always joke that he should have his own website or a T-shirt on that says, 'I'm okay!'"

Comet had been sleeping in front of Dyer's shop, Hymach Industries, since 2002 when he was two years old and had been rescued from a bad situation. Dyer said she couldn't leave the dog at home because he would get anxious and hurt himself, so she would bring him to work with her. "He just feels like this is his corner, and he's good," Dyer told the CBC. "This is just his spot. He's happy and comfortable here, and he's been here all these years."

Comet had been the subject of so many calls to the police and the Society for the Prevention of Cruelty to Animals (SPCA) that they knew him by name, Dyer told 3MillionDogs.com. "Our business is located near a major police station and SWAT team facility. Not only have we had police pull over in regular squad cars to check on the 'dead dog,' but once a fully loaded SWAT vehicle pulled up, officers unloaded in full regalia and checked on the 'dead dog.'

"We will often hear, 'Morning, Comet,' from the community police officers who patrol the neighborhood. Let's just say that Comet is well-known to law enforcement in the area."

He was such a sound sleeper that Comet wouldn't move even when people went up to him to see if he was alive. "People come by and ring the bells on their bicycles to get him to move," Dyer said. "He refuses."

Comet just never got tired of sleeping.

JULIET

SHETLAND PONY

Juliet gave unicorns a bad name when she led police on a four-hour chase through the streets of Madera County, California, in 2016.

The twenty-year-old white Shetland pony was dressed as a unicorn so her owner, professional photographer Sandra Boos, of Fresno, could take pictures of little girls on or next to the horse. For photo shoots, Juliet sported a plush satin horn on her head, a fuzzy pink halter, and a wreath or garland around her neck.

Boos said Juliet made "dreams come true" for little girls who wanted their photos taken with a unicorn. But on one memorable afternoon in 2016, the only dream that the pony wanted to come true was to have free rein. While her owner was preparing for a photo shoot with a group of children in Madera Ranchos, Juliet pulled the lead rope out of a caretaker's hands and bolted.

When Juliet took off, someone had the horse sense to call 911. A disbelieving dispatcher alerted the nearest California Highway Patrol (CHP) officer that a unicorn was running loose. "Initially he thought it might be somebody out there seeing things," CHP spokesman Josh McConnell told the *Los Angeles Times*. "It was a little unreal to hear calls of a unicorn running around on the roadway."

Before the officer arrived on the scene, Boos had captured Juliet. It seemed like a cinch that the drama had ended. But then about two hours later, the pony escaped again. She sparked an all-out chase involving several highway patrol cruisers, local squad cars, and even a helicopter equipped with a thermal imaging device that can detect body heat.

This time, "it was a little more difficult to capture the pony-slash-unicorn," McConnell told the *Times*. It took officers three and a half hours before they found Juliet hiding in an orchard. She was in no mood to give up.

However, the pony's freedom ended when Juliet's pal, a horse named Shady, helped lure her out. Boos said a fellow horsewoman and good friend rode Shady into the orchard. Shady whinnied to Juliet, who whinnied back. "When Juliet saw Shady, she came running," Boos told *USA Today*. To the owner's relief, Juliet followed Shady into a nearby pen for a more stable environment.

"I was standing with the highway patrol when the call came over the radio, and they said, 'The unicorn is in custody,'" Boos said.

Added McConnell, "This was the first call I've ever heard of involving a unicorn."

As for the reason behind Juliet's unbridled adventure, the Shetland pony wasn't talking. She was a little *horse*.

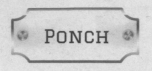

PONCH

CHIHUAHUA

As terrible as rush hour traffic is on the Bay Bridge, which connects San Francisco and Oakland, California, Ponch made it much worse. Police stopped all lanes of traffic while a motorcycle unit tried to catch the little black dog running on the bridge, acting as if this was all a great big game of tag.

Shortly after the morning rush hour got under way one day in 2016, the California Highway Patrol received a call from a motorist that a Chihuahua was on the bridge. CHP motorcycle units went to investigate. The troopers noticed the small pooch on the bridge's north side catwalk (or should that be dogwalk?) heading toward San Francisco.

Fearing the Chihuahua would be hit by a vehicle or cause an accident, officers stopped all traffic, making motorists see red instead of a black dog. A motorcycle officer went over to the little guy to pick him up, but the cute canine bolted onto the westbound lanes of the bridge. That signaled the start of a crazy chase—CHP motorcyclists following a Chihuahua as he scampered across multiple lanes, intent on resisting *a rest*.

Patrol cars joined in the pursuit. The pooch kept zigzagging from officers whenever they closed in on him. Finally, they managed to surround him. While one officer distracted the animal with a jacket, the other came from behind and scooped up the Chihuahua. The chase ended about five minutes after it began.

The dog was taken to the San Francisco Department of Animal Care & Control, where employees named him "Ponch" after Erik Estrada's character, Frank "Ponch" Poncherello, in the TV police drama *CHiPs*.

The actor felt honored the dog was named after him. He tweeted the CHP, "Thank you guys 4 getting that dog off the freeway safe." He added that he had five dogs, including three Chihuahuas.

Ponch, who wore a collar, had no identification or microchip. He was put into foster care while officials waited for his owner to claim him. When no one did, offers to adopt Ponch poured in from dog lovers all over the world after a photo of a CHP officer carrying the Chihuahua and footage of the chase went viral. Officials narrowed the list of potential owners and conducted personal interviews before choosing a family. "Taking into consideration that Ponch is a nervous fellow who loves to run, his new home and family are perfectly suited to give him the happily-ever-after life,"

Animal Care & Control said in a statement. (The family wished to remain unidentified.)

"We're happy that Ponch's story has ended with a loving new home," said Animal Care & Control executive director Virginia Donohue. "We're grateful for all of the good will Ponch has generated for shelter dogs."

★

Honorable Mention: A lone deer halted the morning commute into San Francisco one day in 2004 by bounding across the entire span of the Golden Gate Bridge. Officials said it was likely the first time that a deer, or any other animal, made it safely from one side of the famous structure to the other because it had always been a bridge too far.

At about 8:50 a.m. during heavy traffic, the young deer came down from the coastal wilderness area known as the Marin Headlands. The animal jumped over a concrete wall and onto the bridge, then couldn't figure out how to return home. Now that the deer had come to the bridge, he felt compelled to cross it.

"Before we could get to it and help turn it around, it got out into the lanes," bridge spokeswoman Mary Currie told the *San Francisco Chronicle*. Traffic in the four southbound and two northbound lanes was quickly brought to a halt by the CHP, who wanted everyone to steer clear of the dear deer. In an example of hindsight, a patrol car followed the frightened animal as it galloped across the 1.7-mile span in the southbound lanes.

Once the deer reached the toll plaza area on the San Francisco side, bridge workers tried to capture it, but the animal ran through a FasTrak lane, took the Nineteenth Avenue exit, and disappeared into the woods.

The deer had not only stopped rush hour traffic for twenty minutes, but also had the audacity to avoid paying the toll. Currie told the newspaper that because the deer didn't have a FasTrak payment transponder, the animal "came through as a toll violation, but we will be waiving the [penalty]."

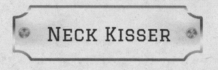

NECK KISSER

BLACK BEAR

Talk about a flirt! A bear came from behind and licked the neck of an unsuspecting woman while she was sitting on a lakeside dock.

Kristen Jones, of Knoxville, Tennessee, was vacationing at her family's house on the shore of Lake James in Nebo, North Carolina, in 2016. She went down to the water's edge to watch the sunrise and do her daily yoga, which she practiced to reduce stress and lower her blood pressure. As part of her morning bliss, she was dangling her feet off the dock and, with earbuds in, listening to music on her cell phone.

Jones thought she was alone. She wasn't. While the woman was gazing out over the serene lake, she was unaware that a black bear was strolling over to her. The bear had no intention of harming her—quite the opposite. He seemed smitten by her. Without even introducing himself, he boldly went up to her and gave her a bear kiss.

"Something sniffed my shoulder, and then I felt something wet along my neck and ear," Jones told Charlotte TV station WJZY. She thought it was the neighbor's dog, but instead of a soft coat, the fur felt prickly and sharp. "I reached up to pet the dog, but it felt weird, so I turned around—and it wasn't a dog. It was a bear!"

Her reaction probably wasn't the one the bear expected. Jones screamed and jumped into the lake, which was understandable for a human who receives an unwanted kiss from a wild bear. Realizing that perhaps he acted a little too forward, the shamed bear headed off in the opposite direction.

"I stumbled backwards into the water, and he ran up the hill," Jones wrote on her Facebook page. "So much for finally being off blood pressure medicine."

Jones told Charlotte TV station WBTV, "The entire thing happened so fast. Sixty seconds and it was done. I was absolutely terrified."

She told the station that despite her initial fear, she immediately started taking photos of the bear "in case something happened, and people found my mauled body." She tailed the bear as he ambled off into the woods.

In addition to taking photos of the four-legged Romeo, she also took a short video of him. "Hey, Bear, where are you going?" Jones said in the video. "You just scared the [daylights] out of me!"

After Jones posted a Facebook account of her up-close-and-personal encounter with the bear, a friend commented, "Next time ask for dinner first."

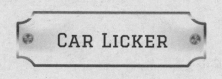

CAR LICKER

MOOSE

Moose can be dangerous beasts. Why, they can even lick the daylights out of a truck or a car. No, not damage the vehicle. Moose can lick one with their tongues.

A couple from Banff, Alberta, Canada, watched a moose give their truck a saliva bath. According to the CBC, Theresa Malan and her husband were driving in

2016 through Peter Lougheed Provincial Park, about eighty miles west of Calgary, when they spotted a bull moose licking another vehicle parked off a snowy road. The moose was slurping the road salt that had stuck to the vehicle.

The moose noticed that Malan had pulled over and was taking photos of him. Having enjoyed the taste of the other vehicle, the moose walked over to the couple's pickup and sampled the salt on their truck. He liked it. For the next half hour, he licked away.

"You could feel his antlers brushing up against the truck," Malan told the CBC. "The moose was very gentle and so chill, and he just had very kind eyes. He didn't have any aggression within him at all. It was a very Canadian experience."

And very *a-moosing* too. The department that oversees the provincial parks, Alberta Parks, issued a safety bulletin that said a moose with a hankering for salt was licking dirty cars in the Rocky Mountain playground of Kananaskis Country. "Please be aware of a moose warning in the Chester Lake and Burstall Pass parking lots and the trails near the lots," said the official notice. "The moose has been very aggressive in approaching vehicles in parking lots to lick the salt from the sides of vehicles."

The warning advised anyone who encountered the moose to honk their horns or sound their car alarm to stop the moose from *a-salting* the vehicle. As if it wasn't obvious enough, the notice added, "Do not attempt to push the moose away from your vehicle while on foot." Like, who would try to push a wild beast that weighs half a ton?

Moose aren't the only ones who crave road salt. Karen Ung tweeted a photo of bighorn sheep stopping traffic in Banff National Park. "The sheep were licking a different car, then approached the one in the photo (as it was still moving!)," she told CritterFiles.com. "Fortunately the driver slowed down and let them wash the car."

No doubt it was a *sheep thrill*.

THE "DUMB BUNNY"

★ MEDALS ★

For making foolish decisions that risked life and limb, the Bad Pets Hall of Shame inducts the following:

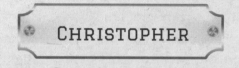

CHRISTOPHER

LABRADOR RETRIEVER

Christopher had never heard the saying, "If you find yourself in a hole, stop digging." So when he found himself in a hole, he kept digging—and nearly got buried in his work.

In 2015, his owner, Kate Geiger, of the New Orleans suburb of Terrytown, let the six-year-old Lab out to play with her other dog, Tayger, in the backyard of the house she had moved into a few months earlier. When she called the dogs to come inside, only Tayger returned.

Geiger told the *Times-Picayune* that she thought

Christopher might have slipped out because he was an adventurous canine who, on a few occasions, had roamed around the neighborhood. She searched the immediate area but couldn't find him.

When she returned home, she heard Christopher's barks, but they seemed muffled. She followed the sounds and discovered they were coming from underneath her concrete patio. "I looked under, and I could hear him, but I couldn't see him," Geiger told the newspaper. "I went and got a light, and I saw him really, really far." The dog had tunneled about twelve feet horizontally under the slab because he really dug his job. When he tried to turn around, he was caught between a rock and a hard place—actually, a piece of cement.

Geiger spent about an hour trying to dig him out. When her efforts failed to rescue him, she called the Terrytown Volunteer Fire Department for help. After hearing about the pooch's dilemma, a crew showed up with shovels. They doggedly dug for the next two hours until they reached Christopher and freed him.

Despite being trapped for such a long time, Christopher was his goofy self when he emerged from the dungeon he had created. He wagged his tail, licked the faces of his rescuers, and even posed with them for a photo.

"He's so happy to be inside, now," Geiger told the paper. "I don't think he's going to go back into that hole."

Yes, Christopher was tired of the *hole* business.

OLLIE

BLACK LABRADOR RETRIEVER

Ollie ended up stranded in the sea after mistaking a lobster-pot buoy for a ball.

The four-year-old Lab swam into deep trouble while fetching a ball with a friend of his owner along an oceanside area known as Rocky Coast near Holyhead, Wales, United Kingdom.

Ollie had been having great fun jumping into the choppy water and retrieving a thrown ball on an August evening in 2016. When the friend hurled the ball as far as he could, Ollie eagerly dived into the sea and swam out to get it. The dog lost sight of the ball for just a moment because of a wave. Once the wave passed, he looked around and spotted what he thought was the ball. Yes, it looked much bigger than the one he was trying to fetch. And, yes, it was red while the ball that he was supposed to retrieve was yellow. But so what? It was a ball!

So Ollie dog-paddled farther and farther out—way past where the tossed ball was floating—and kept his eyes focused on that beautiful large red ball bobbing on the surface more than forty yards from the shore.

Typical of his breed, Ollie was a strong swimmer, so

he soon reached his goal, only to find that the ball was way too big to get in his mouth. Making things more perplexing for him, he couldn't nudge this particular floating ball back to the beach. That's because the ball was a buoy attached to a lobster pot resting at the bottom of the ocean floor.

Disappointed, Ollie decided to head back to shore without his prize. Unfortunately, he snagged his chest harness and collar on the buoy. No matter how much he struggled, he couldn't break free.

The person who had been playing with Ollie noticed the dog was in trouble and thought about swimming out to him. But the water was just too cold and rough, and the dog was too far out. The person then called 999 (the UK's 911) for help. The dispatcher phoned the Holyhead station of the Royal National Lifeboat Institution (RNLI), a volunteer organization of trained water rescuers.

"The lifeboat crew was on the scene in minutes and found the dog, which had been stuck on the buoy for about twenty minutes, tired and beginning to struggle to keep his head above water," the RNLI reported. "As the lifeboat approached Ollie, he turned his head to face the boat, which freed him from the buoy. Despite being tired, he was able to swim back to shore, under a watchful escort from the lifeboat crew."

It all ended swimmingly for Ollie.

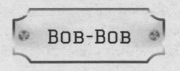

BOB-BOB

MIXED-BREED CAT

Bob-Bob gave new meaning to the phrase "letting the cat out of the bag." He snuggled for a nap in an open suitcase moments before his unaware owner zipped it up. The fourteen-month-old black cat remained trapped in the luggage, which was flown in the cargo hold of a plane, and didn't get freed until ten hours later.

In 2012, the feline's owner, Ethel Maze, of Circleville, Ohio, was getting ready for her annual trip to Disney World with family members and several disabled veterans who lived in her residential-care home. Early on the morning of the flight, she opened her suitcase to add a last-minute item. That's when Bob-Bob hopped in to catch a nap. In her hurry to get to the airport, Maze closed her suitcase without noticing the cat was inside.

"We have a young man who helps out and gets our luggage ready, and he said it looked like a suitcase was moving but he thought he was imagining things," Maze told ABCNews.com. "We had been up all night getting ready, so we thought nothing of it."

After unknowingly packing himself in his owner's

suitcase, Bob-Bob survived an hour ride to Port Columbus International Airport, security screenings and X-rays, and a two-hour flight in a cargo hold. But his ordeal wasn't over. Maze and her group arrived in Orlando too early to check in to their hotel, so they left the bags at the front desk and went out for some fun.

Maze entered her room around 2:30 p.m., about ten hours after she had closed her suitcase. When she opened her bag to hang up her clothes, she spotted something black and furry—something she was sure she hadn't packed. It was her little stowaway.

"I recognized him right away, but I was afraid he'd died because he just lay there," Maze told ABCNews.com. He was lethargic and wet from perspiration. "I picked him up and said to my daughter, 'You'll never guess what. Bob-Bob our cat is with us—in my suitcase.'

"He was so frightened. He hid for about seven hours in our hotel room, and only in the middle of the night did he come out and start licking us and purring."

Maze had to buy a crate, litter box, and food for Bob-Bob, who stayed in the hotel room—and as far away as possible from the suitcase. For the return flight, Bob-Bob flew in his crate in the passenger cabin next to his owner.

He was so happy to be home after his luggage ordeal, he just couldn't contain himself.

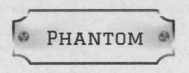

PHANTOM

PALOMINO APPALOOSA

Phantom was responsible for one of the most embarrassing calls ever made to 911: "My horse is stuck in the bathtub!"

The thirty-year-old mare was enjoying some horseplay by dancing around in her stall in Orangeville, California, one day in 2015 when she tripped over an old bathtub that had been converted into her food trough. She tumbled into the tub and landed on her side with all four of her legs up. No matter how hard she wriggled, she couldn't escape from her predicament. She just didn't have the horsepower.

Her owner, Charles Campbell, and his wife tried to free her, but they couldn't budge her or the tub. In desperation, they called 911 for help. "The dispatcher seemed a little confused," Campbell told TV station Fox40 News. "The dispatcher called back a few minutes later and said, 'Your husband can't get out of the bathtub?' And my wife says, 'No, it's my horse.'"

Firefighters from the Sacramento County Metropolitan Fire District were dispatched to the Campbells' ranch to deal with a horse that had fallen into a bathtub and couldn't get up. Using two sturdy

pieces of lumber they had brought, they pried the bathtub sideways, allowing Phantom to slip out. She stood
up and walked away after being stuck in the tub for
twenty-five minutes. Fortunately, she wasn't hurt,
although her ego was probably bruised from the shame
of her silly dilemma.

"This place never surprises me," Campbell told the
TV station.

In a Facebook post, fire officials said, "Now
Phantom can get back to dancing around the stall!"

If she could have answered, Phantom would have
said no, she'll never try that again. She was, after all, a
neigh-sayer.

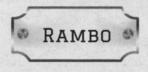

RAMBO

BIGHORN SHEEP

Rambo did something you don't see every day—or ever,
really. He snagged one of his horns on a low-hanging
electrical wire and inadvertently slid partway down a
hill as if he were on a zip line. When he stopped, he
was dangling fifteen feet above the ground, bleating
for help.

It happened in 2009 in the island village of
Helgoysund off the Norwegian coast. Rambo, as he was

nicknamed, was on a hill and, like a wolf in sheep's clothing, wanted to grab the attention of some cute ewes (lady sheep) that were grazing in a field below. He grabbed plenty of attention, but it wasn't the kind he sought.

Without looking where he was going, because he only had eyes for ewes, one of his horns caught a low electrical wire that led to a utility pole at the bottom of the hill. The rambunctious animal became annoyed by this unexpected obstacle and tried to free himself by shaking his head. But that only made matters worse. With his horn firmly caught on the wire, he started to slide down the power line until his hooves were off the ground. The more he squirmed, the more he slid, until he remained suspended high on the wire by a pole near the bottom of the hill.

"My wife saw something surreal from the kitchen window and realized it was the sheep hanging five to six meters off the ground from the wire by its horn. She called me straightaway, asking what to do," Geir Landsnes told the *Daily Mail*. Landsnes and his family were running a small bed-and-breakfast inn next to a sheep farm at the time.

Rambo's bleating caught the attention of several German tourists, who looked up in amazement at the dangling sheep's high-wire act. They and others then mounted a rescue operation. Using ropes and a ladder, they tied the ram's hind legs and pulled him back to the

71

top of the hill, where they were able to free him. Fortunately, Rambo was not harmed by the electrical current running through the wire.

The wired ram's plight was photographed and shared on social media. Had he seen the photos, he would have felt quite sheepish.

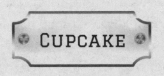

CUPCAKE

SIAMESE CAT

Cupcake picked the wrong place for a snooze.

She hopped into a cardboard box and caught some z's. But when she woke up, she found herself sealed inside it. The box was then sent through the mail and wasn't opened until eight days later.

The laid-back white Siamese was an indoor cat owned by Julie Baggott, of Falmouth, Cornwall, England. In 2016, Baggott had packed a box of DVDs. Before the woman taped it up, Cupcake jumped in and curled up with the DVDs. Not noticing her cat was inside, Baggott sealed the box and shipped it to a customer in Worthing, West Sussex, England, about 250 miles away.

Poor Cupcake remained in the box for eight days without food or water until the package arrived at its destination. Imagine the customer's surprise when she opened the box and found not only the DVDs but a Siamese cat who had taken a package tour. The feline was extremely happy to be released from her cardboard prison.

The customer contacted the RSPCA, which dispatched an agent who picked up Cupcake and took her to Grove Lodge Veterinary Hospital in Worthing. Veterinarian Ben Colwell, who treated Cupcake, told the BBC, "She was quite dehydrated and obviously really quite scared, quite nervous. She's done really, really well. Luckily she was microchipped."

After scanning the cat and discovering the microchip, the vets contacted Baggott. The owner, who had been distraught over the loss of her feline friend, had put up posters and searched around Falmouth for days.

"When I realized she was missing, it was the most horrible, scary feeling," she told the BBC. "We looked everywhere for her. I feel terrible about what's happened. I put everything in the box, and I sealed it straightaway, so I don't know how she managed to get in there. It was a miracle she survived that awful ordeal."

After receiving several days of treatment for dehydration, Cupcake made a full recovery. The mail cat was soon back in the arms of her owner, who happily drove five hundred miles round-trip to retrieve her. Since then, Cupcake always thought outside the box.

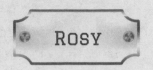

ROSY

YELLOW LABRADOR RETRIEVER

Rosy put a new wrinkle in the expression "up a creek without a paddle." In her case, it was "out toward sea without a paddle."

The six-year-old Lab was frolicking with her owners, teenage brothers Michael and Sean Osborne, of Ullapool, Scotland, on an afternoon in 2015 on the shore of Loch Broom, a lake that leads to the Atlantic Ocean. Eventually, the boys stopped playing with her and went swimming. Meanwhile, Rosy ran off and jumped into the kayak they had left on the water's edge.

When she hopped into the kayak, the impact dislodged it from the shore and it started to float away. She was a smart dog, but not so smart that she knew how to kayak. Of course, it wouldn't have mattered because the paddle was left back onshore.

Although most Labs love the water, Rosy wasn't one of them. She was scared of water and even hated getting wet. There was no way she was going to jump off and swim back to shore. No, instead, she sat in the kayak as the tidal current pulled the craft out toward the Atlantic. She just went with the flow.

While the boys were still in the water, they looked for their dog. To their surprise, they spotted her far out in the lake, her ears down and her head slumped, looking as if she wished she were anywhere else but on a kayak floating toward the sea.

"Rosy hates water, so it just seemed so ridiculous that she was out there on the Loch," the boys' mother, Lisa Osborne, told the *Daily Mail*. "She floated all the way out and basically went as far as the sea.

"It was quite funny, looking back. She made no attempt to jump out to save herself. She just sat in the kayak waiting for the boys to come and rescue her. The boys swam back to shore and got a little rowboat, and then they rowed out using a paddle from the kayak to rescue her."

The dog was out there for about a half hour before being rescued. "Somehow they managed to persuade her to get out of the kayak and jump into their rowboat," Lisa told the newspaper. "She usually can't be persuaded to do anything unless there's food involved. She was fine afterwards. Absolutely nothing fazes her except food. She's quite a character."

Several residents onshore posted photos on social media of the lone mutt on the kayak, according to the Scottish news outlet DeadlineNews.co.uk. Will Goodall Copestake, a kayak instructor, posted on Facebook: "In more interesting news . . . my neighbor's dog just stole his kayak and now seems to be thinking 'this was a bad choice.'"

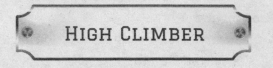

HIGH CLIMBER

MIXED-BREED KITTEN

A stray reached new heights when he climbed an eighty-five-foot water tower. That was a pretty impressive feat for the dark brown kitten. There was just one tiny problem. He didn't know how to get back down.

So for nearly four days, the stranded kitty let everybody know that he was up there and wanted to be down there.

His climbing adventure occurred in LaSalle, Colorado, in 2016. For some reason, he was fascinated by the old water tower that stood over downtown. It had been emptied of water and converted to hold cell phone equipment and antennae. The kitty managed to slip through fencing and began his ascent up one of the tower's ladder-like legs. Apparently, it never dawned on him until too late that however difficult it was ascending the structure, it would be nearly impossible for him to descend safely. He finally figured that out—but only after he had reached, appropriately enough, the catwalk that encircled the water tower tank near the top.

Realizing it was high time to get down, he began mewing for help. Even though he was eighty-five feet from the ground, his plaintive cries were loud enough for townspeople to hear. One day passed, then two, then three. Town officials called Technical Rescue Systems, of Fort Collins, which teaches climbing techniques to rescuers, and asked for help.

"I was, like, 'Absolutely, we're doing that,'" company founder Steve Fleming told the *Greeley Tribune*. He deployed a tactical team to the scene to rescue the feline climber. "It's a little bitty cat," Fleming said. "I don't know how in the world it got up there." He said the LaSalle Fire Department did all the risk-assessment work and set the groundwork for his team.

Under Fleming's direction, climbers Brady Thomas of the Greeley Fire Department and Daniel Winning of the Poudre Fire Authority scaled the tower while a handful of crew members assisted from the ground. The two climbers hauled up a pet carrier. While trying not to spook the freaked-out cat, they coaxed him into the crate. After the rescuers lowered him safely to the ground, twenty onlookers cheered and applauded.

The cat, which appeared to be about six months old and small for his age, was taken to the Valley Veterinary Clinic in LaSalle, where veterinarian Anita Reeve told the newspaper that he was in good shape other than being hungry and thirsty. Given a clean bill of health, the cat was adopted by a family who made a promise to officials that he would be an inside kitty—one, hopefully, who would not need high maintenance.

★

Honorable Mention: Fat Boy, a black-and-white house pet from Fresno, California, scaled a forty-five-foot power pole and wouldn't come down until he was rescued—nine days later!

The cat's owner, Andrew Perez, said he wasn't sure how or why Fat Boy reached the top. The bigger issue was that the cat had no intention of climbing down, even through days of heavy wind and rain. He remained perched on the pole, which was holding a live twelve-thousand-volt line. "We were calling his name, and he was looking at us, and he'd just meow," Perez told television station ABC7.

As the week went by, the family contacted the fire department and other local agencies until officials from the power company Pacific Gas and Electric agreed to help end Fat Boy's high jinks. Because the wires going to the pole were energized, the company had to turn off power to 250 homes in the neighborhood for a few hours.

Two linemen climbed the pole, introduced themselves to the cat, and then wrangled him into the pet carrier they had brought with them. Once he was back on the ground, Fat Boy received nutrients, food, and water from a team from a cat shelter. He appeared in remarkably good health for sitting on a pole for nine days, in what was the ultimate power trip.

★

Honorable Mention: On the Kern County Animal Services's Facebook page, Elizabeth Smith, of Bakersfield, California, recalled how her "goofy little terrier mix" Mamie once chased a squirrel up a fifty-foot oak tree. Smith wrote that Mamie was "jumping from branch to branch like she was a squirrel herself, while I stood at the bottom, astonished, horrified, and helpless.

"And, yep, she got stuck between two large branches. Suddenly remembering that she was a dog, she crouched down and started yelling her lungs out! Fortunately, she attracted the attention of an off-duty fireman, who called the station. They got there in eight minutes, bringing the climbing equipment necessary, [and brought] my crazy 'unsquirrel' down. I bawled like a baby and held her so tightly that she squeaked as the firemen took pictures of us."

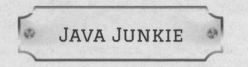
BLACK BEAR

A bear woke up and smelled the coffee—and probably wished he hadn't. He shoved his head into a large empty coffee can and then couldn't get it off.

The bear had been foraging near an old dump about fifteen miles from Tok, Alaska, in 2016 when he found a rectangular metal coffee can. The scent of the coffee was so intoxicating that he jammed his face into the can. Bad move. His head became stuck.

Unable to get his bearings, the coffee-loving beast blindly wandered onto the Alaska Highway. That's when the *brewhaha* began. Surprised motorists had *paws* for concern when they saw a bear with a coffee can over his snout. Cars and trucks braked and pulled onto the shoulder, where drivers stepped out and took pictures of the java junkie, who had a *latte problems bruin*. The driver of a semitrailer stopped in the middle of his lane and watched the bear smack into the truck's wheels.

Randy Rallo, an aviation mechanic who lived in the area, told InsideEdition.com, "The bear walked right past me. He couldn't see. He just kept bumping into the truck. I thought about trying to pull the can from the

80

bear's head, but I gained my common sense and decided against it."

Rallo told the *Alaska Dispatch News,* "Some guy stopped, and he tried to take the [coffee can] off, and the bear swatted at him, and it barely missed him. He walked off and said, 'Let Fish and Game take care of this.'"

Several motorists, including Rallo, had called Alaska State Troopers and local officials with the Alaska Department of Fish and Game. While everyone waited for the wildlife officials to show up, the bear settled underneath the semi and had to "grin and bear it."

About two hours later, Fish and Game agents arrived. After shooting the bruin with a tranquilizer dart that put him to sleep, they used tin snips to cut the empty can off the bear, who they figured was about three years old.

Biologist Jeff Wells told the newspaper that the bear was healthy and in good shape. The animal received an ear tag as well as antibiotics and treatment for the dart wound. The agents put the dozing bear in a pickup and drove him about forty yards into the woods, where he slept until the tranquilizer's effects wore off.

Hopefully, the animal didn't bear a grudge.

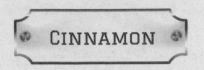

CINNAMON

BLACK BEAR

A bear who was rummaging in a Dumpster suddenly found himself tossed into a garbage truck, which took him for an unintended seventy-five-mile ride.

Nicknamed Cinnamon because of his somewhat rust-colored fur, the one-year-old, eighty-pound yearling was well-known to residents of Grant Grove Village near Hume Lake, California. He often ambled around the little town looking for food and had been "down in the dumps" for months.

In 2015, Cinnamon dived into a Dumpster and was feasting on scraps without paying any attention to the garbage truck that rolled up. Still focused on the goodies he was finding in the trash, the bear tumbled into the garbage truck when the driver—unaware of Cinnamon's presence—emptied the Dumpster. Now inside the truck's compactor, the bear couldn't get out. Cinnamon then took the ride of his life.

"About halfway down the mountains, my truck is going from side to side and I'm thinking it's the road, not knowing I have a bear in my compactor," the driver, identified only as K.C., told Fresno TV station KSEE.

Cinnamon rode in the back of the garbage truck for about seventy-five miles to a dump outside Fresno. K.C. said, "When I dumped the container, I saw all of the employees running. Not knowing why, I pulled forward about ten feet and then I saw Cinnamon running across the parking lot. I was, like, this is not real. A bear in Fresno?"

Far from his home, the yearling had lost his bearings and didn't know where to go or what to do. He just kept running through a south Fresno neighborhood. Police and California Department of Fish and Wildlife employees eventually tracked down the bear and tranquilized him. They examined him and, after finding he was in excellent health, transported him back to the forest near Hume Lake.

"He's one of the local bears," Catherine Cornell, of Grant Grove Village, told the TV station. "I'm sure everyone in the community is happy that Cinnamon is back."

THE "WOLF IN SHEEP'S CLOTHING"

★ PRIZES ★

For brashly intruding into homes and businesses, the Bad Pets Hall of Shame inducts the following:

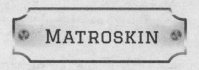

MATROSKIN

MIXED-BREED CAT

When Matroskin was an unnamed hungry stray, she gained worldwide notoriety by sneaking into a fish store and feasting on more than $1,000 worth of seafood.

For several days in 2014, the five-year-old feline had been spotted hanging around Vladivostok International Airport in eastern Russia, looking for a handout. But the workers gave her the cold shoulder, so she took matters into her own paws.

She boldly trotted into the terminal and padded her way straight to a duty-free store that sold expensive gourmet seafood. When no one was looking—other than the shop's security cameras, which recorded her nighttime intrusion—she sneaked inside. Employees went about their work and then closed the store for the night without realizing a trespasser was inside. They locked the doors and went home, leaving the feline all alone.

For a hungry cat, this was a blessing, not a problem. This was a store full of fish for her to consume to her heart's content. She leaped onto an open refrigerated display case packed with every kind of seafood imaginable. Holy mackerel, she didn't *mullet* over for a second. She quickly devoured all sorts of scrumptious morsels from the ocean and didn't even flounder when she pulled a *mussel*.

Security guards spotted her enjoying herself and went into the store, but the cat had such a *shellfish caviar attitude* that she ignored every living *sole* and continued to gorge herself. Somewhat amused, one of the guards pulled out his cell phone and recorded the cat plowing through her seafood buffet. Her evening of gluttony finally ended when the guards kicked her out of the store. She was homeless again, but at least her belly was full.

It was a costly meal for the owner of the shop. She had to throw out all the packages of seafood in the refrigerated case, sanitize it, and restock it. According to the *Siberian Times*, the owner asked the airport authority to cover the loss, but her claim was denied.

When the video of the cat's fish-dining experience was posted on social media, the feline became an instant celebrity in Russia. Many people in Vladivostok offered to adopt her if she could be found. Fortunately for the cat, she wasn't hard to locate. She was still milling around the airport, no doubt hoping to get another chance to sneak into the fish store.

A professional ice hockey team known as Admiral Vladivostok adopted her and made her the club's official mascot. The team even gave her a name—Matroskin, because she reminded players of a feline character with that name in the popular Russian animated feature *Three from Prostokvashino*.

The club's president was so smitten with Matroskin that he announced the team would pay for the fish store's damaged food from the sales of merchandise featuring the cat. Matroskin lived a happy life at the hockey arena, where she was cared for and loved by team officials and players who often were photographed in their uniforms with her.

Sadly, she died just two years later. But that's not the end of the story.

The team wanted to memorialize Matroskin in a special way because she had been special to them. Before the first home game of the 2016–17 season, the club unveiled a bronze statue of their famous feline star outside the arena. The power of Matroskin's memory was as strong as her appetite at the seafood store because in the team's home opener, Admiral beat Vityaz, 5–4.

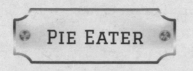

PIE EATER

BLACK BEAR

Oh me, oh pie! A bear broke into a Colorado bakery and gorged on twenty-four pies—and then took two more to go.

The day before the break-in, the bear was photographed by a neighbor of the Colorado Cherry Company, a bakery in Lyons, Colorado, right outside Rocky Mountain National Park. People were always seeing bears in the area, so the owners didn't give it a second thought.

During the middle of the night in 2015, the bear, who had a nose for sweets, smelled those yummy freshly baked fruit pies that were on display inside the shop. He gained access by breaking a window, but he felt no *pane*.

He stuffed himself with "about two dozen pies, bags of cocoa, and a bag of sugar," Mikaela Lehnert, whose mother, Kristi, owned the bakery, told the *Guardian*. For good measure, the intruder took two pies to go.

He exited through the same window he had entered and then ate the two pies outside before waddling off. "I'm looking for servers, so maybe if he wants to come back, I'll give him a job because that's talent to get two pies into the backyard," Kristi told television station Fox31 Denver. "Cherry and apple were his favorite. He passed over the strawberry rhubarb. He wasn't feeling like a tart pie, I guess."

Although the bakery had surveillance cameras, none could bear witness to the *pie-dentity* of the bruin. The cameras were facing a freezer, which contained several more pies, and not the room where the intruder enjoyed his bear fare.

Other than the mess he created in the store and the broken window, there was no damage. Mikaela told the newspaper she was concerned the bear might want to become a repeat customer because he obviously loved their pies. "We have a feeling he knows it's here, so he's going to come back," she said.

Mikaela added this wasn't the first time the owners dealt with a pie-eating bear. Earlier, a bruin broke into their other bakery in Loveland, Colorado, and gobbled up several pies. That intruder did much more damage—breaking a window, the main doors, and the freezer. The invasion spurred the owners to install electrified fences to keep bears out of their garbage.

There was an upside to the bruin's break-in. Mikaela told the *Guardian* that the news reports of the crime boosted their business "because it put our pies and product out there" so the public could see how delicious they were.

★

Honorable Mention: Apparently inspired by the Colorado pie thief, a mama bear and her two cubs broke into a residence in South Lake Tahoe, California, in 2016 and stole two pies that had been baked for a Fourth of July celebration.

Brian Halligan told Sacramento TV station KOVR that when he and his family drove up to their home, they spotted the fleeing burglars. His youngest daughter was the first to notice them. "The littlest one says, 'It's a bear, it's a bear!'" Halligan told the station. "We thought she was kidding, and we turned around and looked, and the mama bear was just coming out in the middle of the road and the two cubs were following her."

The family entered the kitchen and found the bears had trashed it. The refrigerator door was wide open, and food was strewn all over the floor. The bears had come into the house through an unlocked window, wrecking the screen and blinds. It had been easy as pie. They had made their way directly into the kitchen where they opened the refrigerator and then feasted on the Halligans' berry pies and most of the food prepared for the holiday. The bruins ate and ran. As for being caught, they couldn't bear to think about it.

ALLIE

YELLOW LABRADOR RETRIEVER

If Allie had been a human, she would have made a wily safecracker. But she was a dog—a very clever one. During a particularly rascally period in 2014, whenever her owner left for work, Allie would break into the refrigerator and freezer, pull out any morsels that she desired, and eat them.

The yellow Lab had always been a loving, happy dog for her owner, Adam Montiel, host of the local radio show *Up & Adam in the Morning* on Coast 104.5 FM in San Luis Obispo, California. Although Allie occasionally got into mischief, she was obedient and smart. At twelve years old, she proved that you *can* teach an old dog new tricks.

Montiel told ABC News that his girlfriend had taught Allie how to open a drawer containing doggy toys. It didn't take Allie long to apply that newfound skill to other things—like cracking open her owner's double-door refrigerator and its lower one-drawer freezer.

Several times, Montiel would come home from work to a chilling crime scene—refrigerator doors wide open, alarm beeping, and food and containers strewn on the tile floor. Montiel's suspicions clearly focused on his crafty canine and her love for takeout food. There was no question about the motive. Allie was a Labrador retriever, a breed obsessed with food. No, the big question wasn't who did it, but *how* she did it. How was it possible for the dog to open the refrigerator?

In a search for answers, Montiel set up a video camera in an open kitchen cabinet and left the house. When he returned later in the day, he found a recurring sight—an open refrigerator and food on the floor. But this time, he would learn Allie's secret.

When Montiel looked at the video, he was stunned at how cunning and resourceful his otherwise sweet, well-behaved pooch was. The video showed the dog first tipping over the trash can and sticking her head inside to see if there were any interesting things to eat. She came up empty other than some paper that had bits of food on it.

Next, she went to the lower part of the refrigerator that contained the freezer. While standing on her hind legs with her paws on the handle, she backpedaled and slid open the freezer drawer. Then she removed several packages, carried them to a room out of camera range, and ate the contents.

Not satisfied with that haul, the determined pooch returned to the refrigerator and used her paws and jaws to open its double doors near their hinges. Then she closed the freezer drawer with her paws so she could have easier access to the bounty of goodies in the refrigerator. Allie pulled out several containers and even opened one of the storage bins to snare more food.

When Montiel returned home, the camera caught him uttering in surprise, "Oh!"

The radio personality told ABC News that when he saw the video, he was shocked at Allie's ingenuity. "Yeah, I watched it and I was, like, I couldn't believe it," he said. Among the items she stole were a package of tortillas, a package of raw chicken, and dog treats.

Montiel said that Allie never misbehaved as long as he was home. Whenever he left the house, he usually kept her in his room, where she had everything she needed. However, if he forgot to lock the door, she would sneak out and break into the refrigerator.

After the video confirmed Allie was a refrigerator cracker, Montiel made sure to secure the door to his room so the Lab couldn't raid the kitchen. He posted video of Allie's crime on YouTube, and it went viral. By the end of 2016, it had more than 3.3 million views. Her escapade was even featured in a *National Geographic* show about the world's funniest dogs.

"Some people say, 'Oh, dogs don't know shame,'" Montiel told ABC News. "Well, they are wrong. This dog knows exactly what she did."

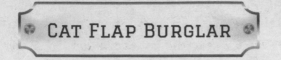

CAT FLAP BURGLAR

BADGER

Not to be outdone by a dog, a wild badger sneaked into a house through a cat flap, broke into a refrigerator, and enjoyed a midnight snack. The intruder did it again the next night, but this time the owner recorded the crime on video.

In the wee hours one morning in 2015, a noise in the kitchen woke up Geoff Taylor, of Midhurst, West Sussex, England. Concerned that a burglar was in the house, he left his upstairs bedroom and crept down the steps. When he entered the kitchen, he noticed the refrigerator door was open. Then came the big shock—the intruder was a badger. The black-and-white culprit had opened the refrigerator, pulled a carton containing half a dozen eggs off a shelf, and then eaten all of them, including the shells. When Taylor confronted the badger, the animal scrambled across the kitchen floor and slipped out through the cat flap.

When criminals find a residence they can break into easily, they often return and burgle it again. The animal was no different. The following night, the critter badgered Taylor a second time.

Awakened by a strange sound coming from downstairs, Taylor grabbed his cell phone and went into the kitchen. He turned on the light and came face-to-face once again with the badger. This time, the trespasser was eating an English pastry known as a Bakewell tart taken from the refrigerator. At first, the badger ignored Taylor and continued to munch on the dessert. But when Taylor took a step closer to the invader, the badger took off running and slipped out the same way it had come in—through the cat flap.

Undeterred even after being scared off, the badger tried to break into the house again a few minutes later, but by that time, Taylor had locked the cat flap.

Taylor's niece, Emma Barrow, shared the video with reporters, including the *Daily Mail*, which dubbed the intruder, the "Cat Flap Burglar." Barrow told the British press, "People often think that badgers are timid creatures that you only see in the garden at night, so this is certainly a shock to see one coming so boldly into a house—especially on two occasions. But we hoped this footage would show people that badgers are real characters, and they can be very bold and cheeky when they get hungry. The way he went through the tart was very impressive. He clearly enjoyed it a lot."

When it came to desserts, the badger really took the cake.

PARTY CRASHER

BLACK BEAR

A black bear crashed a toddler's birthday party. The bruin broke into the tot's house by shattering a skylight and falling into the living room and then ate some sweet treats meant for guests.

Alicia Bishop and Glenn Merrill, of Juneau, Alaska, were making last-minute preparations for their son Jackson's first birthday in 2014. Because guests would be arriving soon, the couple rushed around to put the finishing touches on decorations and food for the celebration.

What the couple didn't know at the time was that a black bear had shimmied up the post of their deck and then climbed onto the roof of their house. The intruder walked over to the Plexiglas skylight above the living room. After he stepped onto the skylight, he looked down and saw a table full of goodies. While the bear was ogling them, the Plexiglas gave way under his weight.

"I was literally in the room, and I heard this cracking," Merrill told the *Juneau Empire*. "And the next thing you know, there's this bear that, I mean, literally, fell right from [the skylight]. It was like three feet away from me." Merrill said he and the bear stared at each other in disbelief. "I don't know who was more stunned. I think both."

The uninvited guest was dazed from the fall but recovered quickly. Merrill's parents, who were visiting at the time, took Jackson to an upstairs room so he would be out of harm's way. Merrill scooted into another room and closed the door. Meanwhile, Bishop, who was in the kitchen, watched the bear through a glass door.

The trespasser calmly wandered over to a table in the living room that held birthday baked goods and helped himself to several lemon-blueberry cupcakes and peanut butter treats.

"The bear walks over and puts his paws up on the table and starts licking birthday cupcakes, and I'm just like, you've got to be kidding me," Bishop told the newspaper. The bear enjoyed the red and green cupcake frosting the most, she said.

After Merrill came out of the room, he and Bishop opened a door that led to the backyard and encouraged the bear to leave by yelling at him. The party animal got the hint and casually walked out the door. Because the bruin acted so calm and showed no signs of aggression, Merrill figured the intruder was used to humans.

The bear loved the cupcakes so much that he wanted back in. He went to the wooden deck and peered inside. "He was up by the window like, 'I want more cupcakes,'" Bishop told the newspaper.

With guests expected to arrive any minute, Bishop

called 911 while Merrill ran next door and borrowed bear spray from the neighbors. He used it on the bruin, who then figured the party, at least for him, was over.

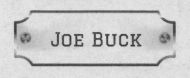

JOE BUCK

DEER

A deer broke into a furniture store that was open for business and did what kids would love to do if given the chance—jump from one bed to another.

It happened at Simpson Furniture in Cedar Falls, Iowa. "I'm still rattled," store co-owner Deb Emmert told the *Waterloo-Cedar Falls Courier* shortly after the 2014 break-in. She was opening the door for a couple of customers when the front window shattered. "I couldn't figure out why the window exploded, if someone shot it out or threw a rock through it," Emmert said. "Someone shouted 'Deer! Deer!' And there was this deer looking right at me and shaking his antlers. He had to be coming pretty fast to break and shatter that. It's tempered glass, and it broke into a zillion pieces."

The deer, estimated to weigh two hundred pounds with possibly a ten-point rack, barely missed knocking Emmert over when he made his smashing entrance. "Someone said, 'Get out of the way!'" Emmert recalled.

"I didn't know which way to go. The guy I was letting in pulled me out the door, and the deer grazed me as he went by."

Bounding over couches and bolting past tables and chairs, the intruder reached the mattress section. The buck stopped there, but only for a moment. Having his own sense of what bedtime meant, he hopped on some mattresses. "He jumped over a queen-sized bed for sure, and he jumped over two sofas back-to-back," Emmert said.

The deer continued his bedlam around the store, causing slight damage to the office and break room and knocking down a mirror with his rack as he passed. Having all the fun he could stand, he went to the back of the store, used his antlers to push open the unlocked rear door, and left. Fortunately, no one was injured by the *deerly* departed.

Employees, who nicknamed the invader "Joe Buck" (after a well-known sportscaster), cleaned up the mess, and the store resumed business. Said Emmert, "We were just laughing, especially when we saw him nonchalantly open the door and just walk out like, 'Okay, I'm done with my shopping.'"

MAMA BEAR

A mama bear wanted to feed her cubs, but because she didn't know how to make lunches, she did the next best thing—she stole them. She broke into an unattended truck and filched the noontime meals of several workers.

In 2015, employees of Squeaky Clean window service had parked their truck at a rural residence in Big Canoe, Georgia, and left their lunchboxes in the cab with the windows down. While the workers were washing the house's windows, they noticed that a mama bear had crawled into the vehicle.

"She was taking lunch to her cubs," Squeaky Clean owner Gilbert Simpson told the *Dawson News*. "She made a few trips in and out of the truck. And then on the last lunchbox, she stayed in the truck and ate it herself and downed three grape sodas. She knew what she was doing."

Once the mama bear and her cubs had polished off the workers' lunches, the bruins ambled off into the woods. The mama didn't damage the vehicle or threaten the workers, but she left them with nothing to eat on their lunch break. They didn't seem to mind, though, because they had a great story to tell.

"My employees came back to the office with smiles on their faces," Simpson said. "They were very happy to feed the bear."

So much for the old saying, "There's no such thing as a free lunch."

★

Honorable Mention: A mama bear and her cub climbed into a woman's parked car and not only ate her lunch and snacks but also tried to steal her purse.

As part of her job in 2015, Kathy Gafford was inspecting a cabin near Gatlinburg, Tennessee, when she looked out and saw two furry intruders in her car. She told Knoxville television station WATE, "The baby was sitting in the passenger seat. The mama was sitting in the [driver's] seat looking like she was cruising around, as if she was fixing to take off. I was carjacked by a bear!

"I've always left my windows down. I just took for granted that they would never get in my car. Well, wrong."

The bruins had taken full advantage of this open window of opportunity.

Gafford, who took pictures of the criminals and

showed them to the TV station, said the bruins devoured her lunch and snacks that had been sitting on the front seat. Then, with her teeth, the mama bear picked up the woman's purse. But because the bear was more interested in food than money and didn't have a great *purse-inality*, she didn't rifle through the handbag.

"Mama was the bad one; she was the bad bear," Gafford said. "She wanted anything and everything she could find in my car."

The bears took off after Gafford made a racket by banging pans together. "She hissed at me a couple of times, and I told her not to talk to me like that."

It was rather unbearable.

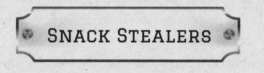

SNACK STEALERS

SEAGULLS

Seagulls have barged into stores in the United Kingdom, taking turns *robin* places of packaged snacks and then *raven* about their *starling* crimes.

According to the British news outlet MailOnLine, in 2016, a seagull flapped its wings in front of the automatic doors of a Greggs Bakery in South Shields, Tyne and Wear, England. When the doors opened, the brazen bird sauntered into the shop. Bemused customer

102

Gordon Lindsay took out his cell phone and videoed the intruder as it waddled down an aisle past a refrigerated display case of drinks and sandwiches to an area that featured snacks.

The seagull then used its beak to snatch a packet of Walkers Squares—a salt-and-vinegar, chip-like snack—off a bottom shelf. The thief didn't care that customers were witnessing the crime. It casually wandered toward the entrance and waited for the automatic doors to open before making its exit.

"I've never seen anything like it," said Lindsay, sharing his video with the media. "I had stopped in to get a bacon sandwich on the way to work, and I could see the seagull was trying to come in. The lady behind the [counter] was having none of it. Then she turned around to fix something on the coffee machine, and the seagull made a break for it.

"The seagull knew exactly how to get the automatic doors to open by flapping its wings, and then it headed straight for the crisps. It had absolutely no shame and certainly didn't hang around once it had got what it wanted. It flapped again to open the doors, and off it went."

The crook was part of a flock of thieving birds of a feather that stuck together to threaten the seaside town. "You can't walk down King Street with food in your hand," Lindsay said. "The seagulls will take it. I've seen them steal stuff in the street, but I've never seen one waltz into a shop and pinch something."

Elsewhere in the United Kingdom, MailOnLine reported that a shop owner felt the need to grouse after winged shoplifters swiped bags of peanuts, chips, and other snacks.

Owner Zaman Iqbal said seagulls loitered outside his twenty-four-hour shop in Aberdeen, Scotland, looking for food. If they couldn't steal any from his customers, the fearless gulls hopped into the store and snatched items off the shelves right in front of startled customers.

Iqbal videoed several of the intruders' crimes and posted them on Facebook. In 2016, he shared a video on social media of a seagull stealing a bag of Golden Wonder BBQ Saucers—a snack similar to a flavored potato chip.

The footage showed Iqbal chasing the sneaky seagull through the aisles before it dropped the bag and made a quick getaway out the shop door. "A customer told me there was a seagull walking around the store," he recalled. "I could hear it rustling with a bag of crisps. It was sneaky, but luckily I managed to chase it off. I just shouted at it, and it dropped the crisps. Then I said 'Thank you.' It flew out of the shop and almost hit a girl who was walking in.

"I've had seagulls come in trying to pinch the snacks for a while now. It's funny but a bit of a nuisance because the seagulls distract the customers as well."

In another video Iqbal took in 2015, a seagull

casually looked around the store before spying a display of nuts. Then it used its beak to steal a bag from a lower rack. The gull tried in vain to open the pack before Iqbal spotted it and shouted, "Get out of my shop!"

Despite his attempts at chasing off the feathered intruders, the gulls kept returning. "Every time they come back, they try to steal something," he lamented.

Yep. The crime wave was for the birds.

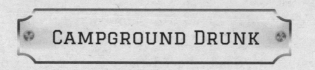

CAMPGROUND DRUNK

BLACK BEAR

A black bear invaded a campground while the campers were on a hike. He didn't mess with their tents or their food. Nope, he went straight for their coolers, which were chock-full of beer.

In 2004, Washington Department of Fish & Wildlife agents found the bear passed out on the lawn of Baker Lake Resort. They figured some sort of trouble had been brewing when they found thirty-six empty cans of Rainier Beer scattered around the slumbering trespasser. The agents realized it wasn't just a snoozing bear. It was a drunken bear.

Based on the condition of the crumpled cans, the

bear used his claws and teeth to puncture them. Although the coolers contained two brands of beer, the bear found only one kind to his liking. "He drank the Rainier and wouldn't drink the Busch beer," Lisa Broxson, bookkeeper at the campground, told the Associated Press.

Fish & Wildlife enforcement sergeant Bill Heinck said the bear barely tried one can of Busch and left the rest of the Busch beer untouched. The three dozen cans of Rainier, which he consumed on a case-by-case basis, hit the spot.

After wildlife agents woke him up, the animal climbed a tree, where he slept it off for another four hours. Agents finally shooed the bleary-eyed, hungover bear away from the campground, but he returned the next morning, looking for another round of drinks.

This time, agents used a large, humane trap and captured him for relocation. For bait, they used doughnuts, honey—and two open cans of Rainier.

THE "PIG OUT"
★ HONORS ★

For devouring things that shouldn't be consumed, the Bad Pets Hall of Shame inducts the following:

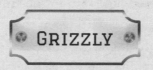

GRIZZLY

CHOCOLATE LABRADOR RETRIEVER

Grizzly was a jewel of a dog—because he swallowed a 2.5-carat diamond engagement ring worth $50,000.

In 2015, his owner, Susan Brewer, of Melbourne, Australia, had left her engagement ring and wedding band on her bedside table before going out. When she returned home, she noticed her band was lying on her bed, and her ring was missing.

With the help of her two sons, Sam and Henry, Susan searched every nook and cranny of the house for the valuable ring but failed to find it. Her suspicions turned toward the family's eight-month-old Labrador. "I was starting to think this naughty dog probably did something with my ring," she told the *Herald Sun*. "But I was hoping he just knocked it around and I would be able to find it."

Knowing how he liked to dig in the flower beds outside, Susan and the boys thought he might have taken the ring and buried it. But a thorough search of his favorite digging spots still turned up nothing. Wondering whether Grizzly ate the ring, Susan called her husband, Mark. They agreed that because their pet was a Labrador—a breed known to eat most anything—they should take him to the animal clinic.

Sure as a diamond sparkles in the sunshine, the mystery of the missing engagement ring was solved. The dog had eaten it. Veterinarian Jessica Ierardo of Greencross Vets took an X-ray of Grizzly's abdomen, which showed the ring in his intestine. Because the vet said the ring wouldn't harm the dog, the family waited for nature to take its course.

That meant they had to go on poop patrol, hoping everything good would come out in the end. Using a plastic knife and fork, Susan examined the droppings every time Grizzly pooped. "I only had to go through two piles of poop to find the ring," she told the newspaper. "[The ring] was very dirty. I put it in boiling water with antibacterial dish soap, and I just kept swishing it." Then she cleaned it with an old toothbrush until it was as good as new and back on her finger—an ending that has a nice ring to it.

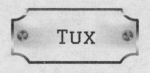

TUX

FRENCH BULLDOG

Tux proved he had very expensive taste—by gulping down his owner's engagement ring.

It happened in 2015 when Jessica Farah, of Miami, Florida, was relaxing at home with Tux and her other dog nearby. "I heard Tux chewing something metal," Farah told Miami TV station WSVN. "At this point, I thought my ring was on my finger. It's a little loose. I didn't realize it had fallen off. I thought to myself, 'He's probably eating his brother's collar. He's always doing that.' And a little later, I look at my hand, and I think, 'Oh no.'" Her ring was gone.

She said that after a search of the house failed to find the ring, she began to think the worst. "It dawned on me, well, I guess it wasn't his brother's collar that he was eating," she said. "It was my ring."

The next morning, Farah took Tux to the Ludlam Dixie Animal Clinic in Miami, where an X-ray confirmed that the case had a familiar ring to it—Farah's, which was inside the dog's stomach. The vets had three options: Wait and hope Tux pooped out the ring, remove the ring surgically, or pull it out through his mouth. They chose the last option. Vets at the Miami

Veterinary Specialists inserted a flexible tube called an endoscope into the dog's mouth, down his throat, and into his stomach. The endoscope had a light source and camera so the doctor could see inside Tux's body. At the end of the device were pincers that grabbed the ring, which the vet pulled out safely.

Once the ring was cleaned and back on her finger, Farah said, "I'm never taking it off—showering, gym, everything. It's never coming off."

Farah couldn't get too mad at Tux because he was responsible for her receiving the ring in the first place. In 2014, the dog ran off. Farah organized a search party, which included a young man who volunteered to help look for Tux. The young man obviously made a good first impression because he eventually became Farah's fiancé and gave her the engagement ring that Tux later swallowed.

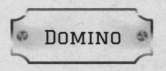

DOMINO

BLACK LABRADOR RETRIEVER

Let's hear it for Domino. The six-month-old puppy ate her owner's hearing aid.

Norma McKenzie, 63, of Charleston, Dundee, Scotland, wore hearing aids on occasion. Whenever she took them out, she put them in a hiding place to keep them from her nosy pet. One day in 2016, she left the house without her hearing aids. Upon her return, she found Domino chewing on one of the devices.

Domino had tried to get her paws on the hearing aids before, but McKenzie had always been able to save them from the pup before they were damaged. Even though the pooch had received a scolding every time she tried to gnaw on them, the reprimands went in one ear and out the other because she continued trying to get at the devices.

On this particular day, McKenzie managed to retrieve a partially chewed hearing aid. But when she couldn't find the other one, she assumed Domino had swallowed it. She knew that the hearing aid could cause a fatal tear or blockage in the dog's digestive system and the battery in the device could burn the pup's stomach lining, leading to serious complications.

Fearing the worst, McKenzie rushed the pooch to the PDSA Pet Aid Hospital. The veterinarians gave Domino a shot to cause her to vomit. "The injection did the trick, and within five minutes, Domino had brought up all the different bits of the hearing aid, along with the battery," McKenzie told reporters. "We also discovered that she'd swallowed bits from a comb and the jewel from a hairclip."

In a PDSA press release, senior veterinarian Andy Cage said, "Dogs, especially puppies and younger dogs like Domino, use their mouth to investigate objects, as well as to eat. Sometimes when doing this, a dog will swallow an object by mistake. Thankfully, Norma brought Domino straight to the hospital, which meant we were able to take action before it caused any serious damage."

Domino made a fast recovery. But McKenzie hadn't heard the last of the dog's appetite for eating inedible things, according to the release. "One day I found her with a pair of my glasses, and one of the lenses was destroyed," she said. "She's also chewed the side of my coffee table. I heard that putting mustard on it would stop her, but she actually enjoyed it and licked it all off! I know she's a puppy and they do like to explore things, but I'm now being a lot more careful where I put things, especially when I get my replacement hearing aids."

At least they were not *ear-replaceable*.

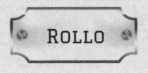

ROLLO

CHOCOLATE LABRADOR RETRIEVER

No chowhound has caused owners more money than Rollo. He was eating them out of house and home.

Because of his limitless appetite, his owners were forced to spend a whopping $38,000 dog-proofing their kitchen. As an uncontrollable eating machine, he wasn't just gobbling food left unattended on the dinner table or counters. Nope. Rollo taught himself how to open the kitchen cupboards, drawers, and refrigerator. He even figured out a way to unlatch the dishwasher so he could lick bits of food off the dirty plates.

His owners, Sue Kirk and Stewart Maher, of Sleaford, Lincolnshire, England, knew what they were in for when they adopted three-year-old Rollo from the Labrador Lifeline Trust in 2009. He already had been adopted and returned to the agency three times by owners who couldn't cope with his nonstop binging.

"He will go to any lengths to get food," Kirk told the *Daily Mail* in 2015. "When I go shopping, I have to bring in one bag at a time and unpack it individually. We always have to make sure we don't leave anything lying around. Rollo is like the terminator—he'll eat absolutely everything. He's constantly on the hunt for food."

Nothing was safe from Rollo's outrageous appetite. He once chewed the plastic lid off a Tupperware container to get at twelve chocolate muffins and then consumed them all. Another time, he unfastened Maher's briefcase and wolfed down the lunch that was packed inside. Rollo ate toast straight from the toaster, devoured a whole package of individual yogurt servings, and consumed a jar of mincemeat—including the glass container—not to mention countless other items.

He could open the refrigerator, pull out food, and gorge himself. "He'd get into the dishwasher, too," Kirk said. "I joked that he was my pre-rinse cycle on the dishwasher. Every time I opened the door to put something in it, his head was straight inside, licking whatever plates he could find."

His owners put up with his eating shenanigans for five years until Christmas 2014 when, in one sitting, he scarfed down five freshly baked Christmas cakes that had been left cooling on the kitchen counter. Having the cakes and eating them, too, left him with a stomachache. He promptly threw up all over Kirk's sheepskin rug.

Kirk and Maher had finally seen enough; they spent the money to remodel the kitchen so Rollo couldn't break into cabinets, cupboards, and kitchen appliances. During the renovation, however, he managed to eat the lunches of two workers and their pack of cigarettes.

The new kitchen had cupboards with handles that Rollo couldn't open, and the fridge was equipped with high pull-handles that the dog couldn't reach. "Everything was specially designed to stop Rollo from getting his paws on the food," Kirk told the newspaper. "We can't stop him from getting at everything."

Efforts to prevent him from pulling apples off their backyard tree were fruitless. They could never get to the core of the problem. "He loves apples; they're his favorite, and he'll do anything for an apple," Kirk said. "There are never any apples for us to eat because he stands up on his back legs and shakes the tree until the apples fall down. He's even bounded onto the trampoline and bounced up and down to get at the apples."

To Rollo, eating vegetables couldn't be *beet*; he didn't *carrot all* what he ate. He once chomped on twelve cauliflowers from the garden. Unfortunately, most of the veggies he tried to consume were from Kirk's greenhouse. The owners set up a child safety gate to prevent him from breaking in there. "He'll body-bash it to get at the tomatoes," she said. "We've put a chain on the door after he learned to open it, and we've got Rollo-proofed bins to stop him from rummaging.

"The only things he doesn't really like are onions and celery, but anything else is fair game. We've spent thousands over the years on vet bills after he's eaten everything from glass to rat poison. He causes absolute mayhem, but we love him to pieces."

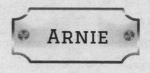

ARNIE

BEAGLE

Arnie had a strange fascination with historical figures such as Benjamin Franklin, Ulysses S. Grant, Andrew Jackson, and Abraham Lincoln. He was extremely fond of their portraits. On money. Which he ate.

His total consumption? Four hundred and fifty dollars.

In 2005, when he was three years old, Arnie devoured $150 in cash that his owners, Corey and Hope O'Kelley, of Largo, Florida, had left out on a coffee table. The money had been a gift from Hope's father. Luckily, the couple managed to recover two fifty-dollar bills—which had a portrait of Grant on them—after the cash had traveled through Arnie's digestive tract and ended up in his poop. It was dirty money.

The beagle's appetite for raw currency diminished for several years until 2012 when he once again developed a taste for greenbacks. Hope's father had given her cash, this time $300 in various denominations, for swimming lessons for the couple's three-year-old daughter. The money was inside an envelope, which was inside Hope's wallet, which was inside her purse, which sat on top of the kitchen table.

Sometime during the night, while his owners were sleeping, Arnie jumped onto a kitchen chair and then onto the table. The scent of Jackson on the twenty-dollar bills and Lincoln on the five-dollar bills was just too tempting to ignore. Sticking his head in Hope's open purse, Arnie pulled out her wallet and carefully removed the cash-stuffed envelope. Savoring the taste of money, the beagle dined on the dough and became a canine cash cow.

The next morning, Corey walked into the kitchen and noticed the purse was open and so was the wallet. Then he spotted a twenty-dollar bill and a five-dollar bill. "The five had been chewed on a little bit, and so I didn't think much of it," he told Bay News 9, a local cable station. "I figured my wife had a few bucks in her wallet [that Arnie had taken]. Then she came flying out of the bedroom, saying, 'Oh no! Oh no!' She started going through her purse and realized that the dog had eaten all of it except for that twenty and that ripped-up five."

It was pretty obvious that the remaining $275 were tucked into Arnie's belly.

"I realized pretty quickly that it wasn't as funny as I first thought it was," Corey told the *Tampa Bay Times*. Hope said she was shocked by Arnie's sneaky gluttony, telling the newspaper that he must have been able to smell her father's money. She was unaware of any particular resentment the beagle harbored toward her dad. The dog just had this thing for her father's dough.

The couple now had a cash flow problem. They followed Arnie around for a week, going through his poop and picking out pieces of money, which he had shredded before swallowing. They washed the tattered cash and put several pieces back together. Perhaps feeling guilty, Arnie helped them by puking up some of the money in more easily washable form.

With help from relatives, Hope found enough pieces of each bill to show a complete serial number. She took the money fragments to a bank, which agreed to replace the bills with new ones, much to the relief of the O'Kelleys.

As for Arnie and his costly late-night snack, it seemed money didn't bring that much happiness.

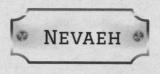

NEVAEH

DOBERMAN PINSCHER

Nevaeh let everyone in the household know how much she liked rich food—by devouring a $4,100 check.

Her owner, Jeff Vogelgesang, of Massillon, Ohio, bought the dog as a Christmas present in 2007 for his girlfriend, Lisa Wood, and her son, Justin. Vogelgesang named the pup Nevaeh, which is *heaven* spelled backward, but the canine was sometimes just the opposite. Within the first couple of months, she had chewed belts, a computer cord, and a dental retainer.

Later that spring, Vogelgesang, a truck driver, was on the road when he told Lisa and Justin to be on the lookout for a $4,100 check that was due to arrive in the mail from the IRS—a tax refund.

"I knew the check was coming," Vogelgesang told the *Independent*, the local newspaper. "I told them two weeks earlier to make sure they put the mail up because she was starting to get into things."

When Justin arrived home from work, he picked up the mail and left it on the kitchen table. Later that evening, Vogelgesang called home to see if the check had arrived. Justin told him that the dog had climbed onto the table and tore into the mail. Barely able to make out the return address on one of the ripped and shredded envelopes, Justin figured out it was from the U.S. Department of the Treasury, the agency that oversees the IRS.

"I reacted like anyone whose dog ate a $4,100 check," Vogelgesang told the *Independent*. "I said, 'Oh my God, no!'"

Justin told the paper, "I put [the mail] on the kitchen table, right in the middle. She's so little so I don't see how she could've gotten up and grabbed it." But she did, and she ate it—a true gut check.

"I've got a $4,100 dog right now," Vogelgesang joked at the time. "She's a devil." Seeking a replacement check, he called the IRS. After the representative stopped laughing at the dog-ate-my-check tale of woe, he directed Nevaeh's owner to a department that handles claims for lost or damaged checks. Vogelgesang eventually received a new check.

"I was half tempted to run around with a pooper scooper through the yard to try to retrieve the dollar amount, but I thought I'd just wait the six to eight weeks," he said. "She had to eat my check. She couldn't eat the gas bill, the electric bill, or anything else."

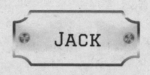

JACK

JACK RUSSELL TERRIER

Jack had plenty of common cents, but not much common sense. That's because he ate 111 pennies.

"He'll eat anything he can, whether it's garbage or whatever," owner Tim Kelleher, of Manhattan, told TODAY.com in 2013 shortly after his thirteen-year-old pet chowed down on the coins. "He was trying to get into a bag of bagels and knocked over the change on my desk. When he went to lick up the crumbs, he licked up the pennies at the same time. Then 111 pennies later . . ." To coin a phrase, it was *mint* to be.

At the time, Kelleher wasn't aware of Jack's sudden taste for pennies. But when the dog began vomiting, the owner rushed him to BluePearl Veterinary Partners. Because the pennies contained a lethal amount of zinc that could destroy Jack's kidneys and liver, veterinarian Suliman Al-Ghazlat performed emergency surgery. He methodically removed the coins five at a time in an operation that took two hours and cost a pretty penny.

"Jack is more than okay," Kelleher said after the surgery. "He's right back to himself. He's loving all the attention and jumping all over the place."

And what happened to all those pennies? Kelleher told Dr. Al-Ghazlat, "Keep the change."

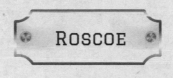

ROSCOE

MIXED-BREED DOG

You've no doubt heard a student claim, "The dog ate my homework." Well, Roscoe is living proof that sometimes the excuse is actually true.

The five-year-old pet of Reagan Hardin, of Magnolia, Texas, was watching her build a model of a Middle Ages farm for her advanced placement world history project. Working for hours in an upstairs room in 2014, the Magnolia West High School sophomore glued plastic sheep, horses, chickens, cows, pigs, fences, structures, and trees on a large, square board. She even built a wire fence around the farm.

The day before Reagan was to turn in her work, Roscoe took great interest in the project and found the little plastic animals irresistible. You can bet the farm over what happened next. When no one was looking, the dog ate the animals and, for good measure, bit into sections of the metal wire fence. He then tore the project to pieces before trotting off.

When Reagan's mother, Kristen Barker, went upstairs and saw the girl's farm in ruins, she knew immediately who to blame. But her aggravation turned to worry once she realized that the plastic farm animals were missing, leading her to believe Roscoe had consumed them. She rushed Roscoe to an emergency animal clinic, which confirmed, through X-rays, that the dog had a stomach full of Reagan's homework. This was no laughing matter because the objects posed a hazard for the dog.

Roscoe was transferred to the internal medicine specialists at North Houston Veterinary Specialists, where they removed the objects from his stomach one by one with an endoscope rather than through surgery. The dog made a quick recovery.

Pointing to an X-ray of the items that he had pulled from Roscoe's belly, veterinarian Carl Southern told KHOU-TV, "You might be able to see half of a horse body, a sheep, a chicken head. I kept seeing a little pink horse body go by, but it ended up being a pig with a curly tail."

Once everything was removed from Roscoe's stomach, Dr. Southern sent an image of the X-ray to Reagan, who needed it to prove she had a valid excuse for not turning in her project on time. The girl told the TV station, "My teacher thought I was joking, so I showed her [the X-ray] and she said, 'So your dog really did eat your homework?' I said, 'Yes, he was in the emergency room.'"

Reagan was given extra days to make a second Middle Ages farm for her homework assignment. This time, she kept it out of Roscoe's reach.

"Don't put anything past your dog," said Dr. Southern. "You always hear people say, 'My dog would never eat that.' Well, that's often the main thing he will eat." Roscoe was the perfect example.

★

Honorable Mention: A Great Dane socked it to his owners. They couldn't figure out why their socks were disappearing. They found their answer after he became sick and began barfing.

His owners, who asked to remain anonymous, brought him to the DoveLewis Emergency Animal Hospital in Portland, Oregon. After taking X-rays of the canine, the vets found a large quantity of foreign material in the Great Dane's belly. Unsure what he had consumed, the vets performed exploratory surgery and were stunned when they removed forty-three socks. (It's not known how many were matches.) According to ABC News, veterinarian Ashley Magee, who performed the three-hour operation, recalled, "I just was pulling out sock after sock after sock." The three-year-old dog made a speedy recovery and went home the next day.

His case won third place in the *Veterinary Practice News*'s 2014 "They Ate What?!" X-ray contest.

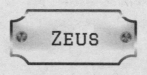

ZEUS

DOBERMAN PINSCHER

Zeus was a champion ball hog.

He loved to chase after the golf balls that his human family hit in the backyard. The problem was that he didn't retrieve all of them. Some he ate—until more than two dozen filled his stomach.

When the one-year-old dog went *ball-istic*, he became increasingly sick, so his owners brought him to the Lisbon Veterinary Clinic, in Lisbon, Ohio, where the staff examined Zeus, did some blood work, and took X-rays.

"The staff reported that something, well, didn't look right," Dr. Gordon Schmucker told *Veterinary Practice News*. "You have at least one second of, 'What's wrong with the X-ray machine? What did the dog eat? What's going on? That can't be real!' But then you realize, 'Hmm, that's real!'"

The X-rays didn't lie. Zeus had a belly full of golf balls. Exactly how many wasn't determined until Dr. Schmucker operated on him and extracted twenty-six golf balls. The vet then broke the news to the owner, who wasn't all that surprised. "The guy told me that the dog chases golf balls," Dr. Schmucker recalled. "He and the kids hit golf balls [in the backyard]." The owner hadn't mentioned anything about golf balls prior to the operation.

The vet told the publication that he had removed a golf ball or two from dogs before, but he had never seen a canine's stomach with so many in it. "It's not something we do every day," he said. The bizarre case left Dr. Schmucker with some questions: First, why does a dog do that? And, secondly, how did Zeus manage to hold so many golf balls in his tummy before showing signs of distress? Apparently only when the dog consumed twenty-six did he get sick.

Zeus recovered quickly and didn't return to the vet for further golf ball issues. But his legacy will last because his case won top honors in the *Veterinary Practice News*'s 2015 "They Ate What?!" X-ray contest.

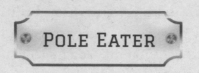

POLE EATER

BLACK LABRADOR RETRIEVER

A ten-week-old stray puppy found a fishing pole and caught nothing but trouble. No one knows why, but the dog swallowed a section of the pole that was more than half his size.

A Good Samaritan in Tulsa, Oklahoma, picked up the homeless puppy after seeing the dog was sick and throwing up. The black Lab was brought to an emergency animal clinic and then transferred to Woodland West Animal Hospital, where he was examined by veterinarian Mike Jones. The dog looked depressed and kept sticking his neck out and vomiting.

"When I was looking at the puppy, I could see a little something in the back of the throat but I couldn't tell what it was," Dr. Jones told *Veterinary Practice News*. "When I took the X-ray, it was like, 'Holy cow!'" The dog had swallowed a fishing pole—which certainly caught the veterinarian by surprise.

Dr. Jones sedated the puppy and then gently pulled the pole out with retrieval forceps. There was no need for surgery. "As soon as he woke up from the sedation, we gave him a bowl of food and he was perfect."

"We see a ton of dogs and cats eating fish hooks because a hook smells like bait, and the bait looks like a bug," said Dr. Jones. "There is a reason why dogs and cats want to try to swallow those." But a fishing pole? In *Veterinary Practice News*'s annual "They Ate What?!" contest, the *reel*-life case earned second place in 2015.

In a way, the fishing pole helped the stray dog catch a break. After his recovery, he was turned over to a rescue group, which found a loving, forever home for him.

ABOUT THE AUTHOR

Allan Zullo is the author of more than one hundred nonfiction books on subjects ranging from sports and the supernatural to history and animals.

He has written the bestselling Haunted Kids series, published by Scholastic, which is filled with chilling stories based on, or inspired by, documented cases from the files of ghost hunters. Allan also has introduced Scholastic readers to the 10 True Tales series about people who have met the challenges of dangerous, sometimes life-threatening, situations.

As an animal lover, he is the author of such books as *The Dog Who Saved Christmas and Other True Animal Tales; The Dog Who Saved Halloween and Other True Animal Tales; Bad Pets: True Tales of Misbehaving Animals; Bad Pets Save Christmas! True Holiday Tales; Bad Pets Most Wanted! True Tales of Misbehaving Animals; Bad Pets on the Loose! True Tales of Misbehaving Animals; Miracle Pets: True Tales of Courage and Survival; Incredible Dogs and Their Incredible Tales!; True Tales of Animal Heroes;* and *10 True Tales: Surviving Sharks and Other Dangerous Creatures.*

Allan, the grandfather of five and the father of two grown daughters, lives with his wife, Kathryn, near Asheville, North Carolina. To learn more about the author, visit his website at **www.allanzullo.com.**